Mother Goose Comes First

LOIS WINKEL
and SUE KIMMEL

Mother Goose Comes First

An Annotated Guide to
the Best Books and Recordings
for Your Preschool Child

HENRY HOLT AND COMPANY • New York

NEbF

Library of Congress Cataloging-in Publication Data
Winkel, Lois.
    Mother Goose comes first : an annotated guide to the best books
    and recordings for your preschool child /
    by Lois Winkel and Sue Kimmel.
    ISBN 0-8050-1001-7
    1. Children's literature—Bibliography.   2. Bibliography—Best
books—Children's literature.   3. Children's literature—Juvenile
sound recordings—Catalogs.   4. Preschool children—Books and
reading.   I. Kimmel, Sue.   II. Title.
Z1037.W777   1990
[PN1009.A1]
011.62—dc20   89-26833

Printed in the United States of America
Recognizing the importance of preserving
the written word, Henry Holt and Company, Inc.,
by policy, prints all of its first editions
on acid-free paper.

10 9 8 7 6 5 4 3 2

To D.Z.C.H. even though he's aged out.
And to K.A.J. because she's just beginning.
—L.W.

To the Three Js.
—S.K.

Contents

Introduction

Most parents, even brand-new ones, know that reading to preschool children is important. What is less clear is what to read, why read, and when to read.

What to Read

With over three thousand five hundred children's books published per year and over fifty thousand currently in print, it is quite a task to sort out the good and superb from the far more numerous mediocre and outright dreadful.

It seemed strange to us that with the tremendous increase in publishing for very young children over the past decade, there was not a comprehensive guide to books and recordings for parents and caregivers. There are other lists of children's books, but most encompass childhood from early years through the age of twelve. It goes without saying that broader works cannot include as many titles for each audience segment. The few targeted for preschoolers do not include the full range of titles that are available and appealing to young children. The organization of these works has also seemed curious. Age is not the exclusive factor in determining the appeal of a book or recording. Subject or theme is more likely to be.

Just as in any other field, it helps to know the product and the user. We've spent over thirty years working with children in a variety of settings: play groups, nursery schools, inner-city classrooms, and urban and suburban libraries. As the former editor and bibliographer of *The Elementary School Library Collection,* an evaluative collection development guide for school and public libraries, we've also spent over a dozen years reading 99% plus of all children's books published, and listening to recordings produced for them. We've lived with children—our own—and while, thankfully, they are too few in number to constitute a scientific study, they and their friends and classmates have increased our understanding of what works well.

While infants start with Mother Goose's nursery rhymes, they are soon ready for more. What they want—stories, poems, folktales, songs, information, or identification books—in large part should be up to them. Since they do not know what is available, but do know what they like, children need adults to pick up cues from their behavior or their reactions to activities and things they see.

Mother Goose Comes First is intended to be a practical and usable guide. It is organized by broad genre or subject themes because children are adamant about their preferences. Each entry shows the author, title, illustrator, publisher, and availability in hardcover or paperback bindings. All books are in print as this book goes to press. A brief description of the work follows and the typical age range of appeal is shown in parentheses. These are not meant to be restrictive. (The age annotation of 5 means the book is suitable for the upper end of the preschool scale and may be suitable for older school-age children also.)

If a child is strongly interested in a subject or theme for an extended period, that sustained interest will hold through materials usually considered appropriate for an older child. Often too, an older child will go back to a book that was a favorite months or even a year or two earlier. Young children need to exercise their prerogative of choice at times, just as adults do. By respecting children's choices, adults confirm reading as a valid and valued activity for them.

Sometimes a recording of the work is available and has been noted. When that recording has turn-the-page signals and is packaged with the book, it is identified as a read-along kit. Certainly, recordings do not always have to come pre-packaged; parents can make their own. Recorded books are helpful on two fronts: to spare parents who've grown weary of a particular favorite, and to give toddlers and pre-schoolers greater choice of when to hear a beloved book. Recordings of songs and singing games are also included.

There are two indexes. One lists authors, illustrators, and performers, to help you find other works by favorites. The other cites titles, to help you locate specific works.

We suggest you browse through the book to get a sense of the scope of the recommended titles. Then use it section by section, depending on the child's known interests and current activities. Do choose titles from other sections occasionally to see if interest has changed and to insure exposure to the wider range of available titles.

Reading is one of the best ways to satisfy the itch known as human curiosity. Young children are innately inquisitive. They ask what seems like hundreds of questions—daily. There is a largely undiscovered wealth of attractive books that give information at their level. The often untalked-about plus of reading such information books is that the adult's knowledge is refreshed or even enhanced.

In choosing and using books, remember:

Tone is critically important. Even quite young children lose interest when they sense they are being patronized.

Illustrations in all techniques are appreciated: drawing, painting, collage, and photographs, in black and white as well as full color, and simple or complex in style.

The age of the book or recording doesn't matter—seventy-year-old classics can work just as well as a contemporary book.

Production quality is important. Young children do notice when the illustrations or text on one side of the page show through the reverse page.

Reading aloud shouldn't become a testing situation. Be open enough to answer questions that arise, but don't constantly ask children questions about the books you've read to them.

All children do not like all books. They're not supposed to like all books—even if those books are classics. (And even if you liked them as a child!)

All books do not have to last forever. Reading does.

Why Read?

Early childhood, from birth through the age of five, is that very special time spent achieving mobility, learning to talk, and gaining information.

While reading to infants, toddlers, and preschoolers doesn't help with their mobility (except when used as a resource for fingerplays and action games and songs), it certainly contributes to their language development, their ability to concentrate, their motivation for wanting to learn to read. And it helps answer their constant questions.

Interest in subjects and types of books will vary. As children develop, the language in different books will make different demands on the reader/listener. Higher-level critical reading/listening skills develop earlier than might be expected. The introduction to good literature of all types begins to set the standards that will be used throughout life.

There is a direct and positive correlation between a child's vocabulary, sentence structure, and writing style, and his exposure to literature. Mobility and talking are dependent largely on muscle development. Toddlers have a passive vocabulary before their tongues lift to form "Da." They continue to know more words than they can say. As youngsters who've been read to begin to speak fluidly, they have a larger vocabulary and form more complex sentences than children who have not been exposed to reading. They also are on the first step to becoming independent readers.

One of our most consistently reassuring observations has been of the love all children everywhere have for books once they know what they are and what they can do. Three factors are most important in promoting a child's desire to read. Reading to your child is first. Books in the home, whether they are borrowed from the library or owned, is second. And parents and other adults seen reading for their own purposes and pleasure is third.

Reading is not a skill picked up with a mere snap of the fingers. Learning to read is a complex task that requires considerable concentration. A child who is motivated to learn to read will put forth the effort to learn to read. Just as muscular maturity plays a large part in moving and talking, physiological and emotional maturity play a large part in being able to read. There is no reason to push children to read early. There is every reason to read to them.

When to Read

Reading just before naptime or bedtime is a tradition. Children don't normally like naptime and bedtime. Restricting reading to those times carries a subliminal message: reading is a soporific. That's not the message we want to convey. Reading needs to be a mainstream, typical part of the day's activity. Reading needs to be shown to be an exciting rather than lulling experience. It is a wonderful way to start the day. It is a wonderful dessert after dinner. It is a spirit refresher anytime. Integrate reading with daily or special activities: family trips, walks, planning a birthday party, going shopping. Reading, like anything else, gains more meaning through use. You and the child will enjoy reading whenever and wherever you do it.

Nursery Rhymes and Lullabies

For generations adults have held babies in their laps and sung, recited or read many of the selections from titles in this section. Mother Goose comes first because these rhymes are the corner-stone of literature and cultural heritage for the young child. They constitute the primary introduction to the rhythm, texture, and flexibility of language.

Some of the Mother Goose collections are more extensive than others. The choice of which to select is really a personal one. Remember that to an infant, rhythmic sound and rhyme repetition are more important than illustrations. Learn to sing or chant the rhymes. Changing a diaper or dressing a baby, mealtimes, riding in a car all become easier. Soon small voices chime in or request a favorite.

Toddlers and preschoolers pay more attention to pictures in books than do infants. Looking at different illustrators' interpretations begins children's visual aesthetic awareness.

- Berman, Marcia. **Marcia Berman Sings Lullabies and Songs You Never Dreamed Were Lullabies.** B/B Records, 1989. (Record/ cassette) ○ ▣

  A unique and varied selection of a dozen songs, from the jazzy "Pajamas" to the traditional "Raisins and Almonds" and the vintage "Lullaby of Broadway." The voice is clear and versatile whether a cappella or accompanied by any one of a number of instruments. Babies and very young children enjoy the soothing quality of the music, and older listeners delight in the departure from the usual lullaby fare.

  (0–5)

- Briggs, Raymond. **Mother Goose Treasury.** Dell (p) 1980. 224p illus.

  More than four hundred rhymes are brilliantly illustrated with over eight hundred pictures in color and black and white. The index of first lines is wonderfully helpful. Be prepared to buy more than one copy. This comprehensive edition gets very heavy use for several years.

  (0–5)

- Buck, Dennis. **Singable Nursery Rhymes.** Kimbo 1986. (Record) ○
  Join in singing these traditional Mother Goose rhymes. *(1–5)*

- Caldecott, Randolph. **A First Caldecott Collection.** Warne 1986. 64p col and b&w illus.

  *Comfortably fitting into a young child's hand, each of these three small books—***A First Caldecott Collection: The House That Jack Built and A Frog He Would A-Wooing Go; A Second Caldecott Collection: Sing a Song of Sixpence and Three Jovial Huntsmen;** *and* **A Third Caldecott Collection: Queen of Hearts and The Farmer's Boy—***includes two favorite Mother Goose nursery rhymes with Caldecott's nineteenth-century, charmingly detailed, vivacious illustrations.* *(0–5)*

de Angeli, Marguerite. **Marguerite de Angeli's Book of Nursery and Mother Goose Rhymes.** Doubleday (h&p) 1954. 192p col and b&w illus.

This large collection of nursery rhymes is softly illustrated throughout in black and white with several full-page pastel-hued drawings. (0–5)

- Cauley, Lorinda Bryan. **The Three Little Kittens.** Putnam (p) 1982. unpaged col illus.

Young children readily identify with the predicaments the three hapless kittens find themselves in. This familiar verse is illustrated by charming, quaint drawings filled with detail. (0–3)

- **Golden Slumbers: Lullabies from Near and Far.** Harper Audio, 1972. (Record/cassette) ● ☷

The songs on this recording have been sung to children for centuries. The voices of Oscar Brand, Pete Seeger, Jean Ritchie, and many other folksingers capture the songs' original flavors while illustrating their continuing ability to soothe and enchant the listener. (0–5)

- Greenaway, Kate. **Kate Greenaway's Mother Goose.** New York Public Library/Metropolitan Museum of Art/Dial 1987. 3 books boxed. unpaged col illus.

A set of three board books, each with five Mother Goose rhymes, is accompanied by Kate Greenaway's quaint nineteenth-century illustrations. An extremely attractive format and design. (0–3)

- Hague, Michael. **Mother Goose: A Collection of Classic Nursery Rhymes.** Holt 1984. 61p col illus.

Selected and illustrated in imaginative detail by the artist with his own children in mind, this collection is a gorgeous work of art. (0–5)

- Hale, Sara Josepha. **Mary Had a Little Lamb.** Illus. by Tomie dePaola. Holiday (h&p) 1984. unpaged col illus.

  Richly colored illustrations accompany the classic poem set to music describing the adventures of a young girl and her pet. (0–5)

- Harrop, Beatrice, editor. **Sing Hey Diddle Diddle: 66 Nursery Rhymes with Their Traditional Tunes.** Illus. by Frank Francis and Bernard Cheese. A. & C. Black (dist. by Sterling), 1983. unpaged b&w illus.

  This collection provides piano arrangements and guitar chords for 66 traditional nursery rhymes. Its spiral binding allows for easy use on the piano. (0–5)

- Herdman, Priscilla. **Star Dreamer: Nightsongs and Lullabies.** Alcazar Productions 1988. (Cassette) ▪▪

  An outstanding collection of nighttime music sung in a beautiful clear voice. Includes a diversity of music and lyrics from Raffi to Brahms to Robert Louis Stevenson. (0–5)

- Ivimey, John W. **Three Blind Mice.** Illus. by Paul Galdone. Clarion 1987. unpaged col illus.

  While the short version of the song is best known, in 1917 Ivimey wrote an extended version providing an explanation of the reason for, and the aftereffects of, that stanza. The edition currently available features double-page-spread watercolor paintings. The musical score for piano is on the back cover. (0–5)

- Jack, David. **Don't Wake Up the Baby.** Lyrics by Susan Jack. Music by David Jack. Ta-Dum Productions 1987. (Cassette) ▪▪

  Original lullabies for nap and bedtime comprise this outstanding collection. The melodies are wonderfully hummable, and both male and female voices are used on the recording. A Spanish-language version is also available. (0–5)

- Lobel, Arnold. **Random House Book of Mother Goose.** Random House 1986. 176p col illus.

  Uniquely and exuberantly illustrated in watercolors, this edition combines familiar and unfamiliar rhymes. (0–5)

- **Lullabies for Little Dreamers.** Performed by Kevin Roth. CMS 1985. (Record/cassette) ⊙ ▭

  A dulcimer provides the accompaniment to this selection of gentle, reassuring lullabies. (0–5)

- Potter, Beatrix. **Beatrix Potter's Nursery Rhyme Book.** Warne 1984. 59p col illus.

  Familiar and newly-created nursery rhymes are joined with the illustrator's beloved trademark pastel watercolors of animals in this gentle collection. (1–5)

- Potter, Beatrix. **Cecily Parsley's Nursery Rhymes.** Warne. 34p col illus.

  "Goosey Goosey Gander" and "This Little Pig Went to Market" are two of the verses illustrated with the drawings of Beatrix Potter in this small book. (0–5)

- Provensen, Alice and Martin. **Old Mother Hubbard.** Random House (h&p) 1977. unpaged col illus.

  Each time Old Mother Hubbard goes out to get something for her dog, she returns to find him engaged in some unpredictable, often silly activity, such as dancing a jig. The pages turn to reveal each of the dog's new tricks in humorous illustrations.   *(1–5)*

- Spier, Peter. **London Bridge Is Falling Down!** Doubleday 1967. unpaged col illus.

  Detailed drawings of London Bridge, its construction, and the shops and streets of eighteenth-century London accompany the text of this familiar song. Musical notation is included.   *(0–5)*

- Spier, Peter. **To Market! To Market!** Doubleday 1989. unpaged col illus.

  A collection of traditional nursery rhymes begins with morning on the farm, moves into town for market, and then goes back home at the end of the day. Illustrated in detail with authentic scenes from nineteenth-century America.   *(2–5)*

- Stevens, Janet. **The House That Jack Built.** Holiday 1985. unpaged col illus.

  The rat eating the malt that lies in the house that Jack built starts a cumulative chain involving a cat, a dog, a cow, a maiden, a man, a priest, a cock, and a farmer, all captured in large, humorous pictures.   *(1–5)*

- White, Ruth, and David White. **Sing Along with Mother Goose.** Rhythms Production 1983. (Record/cassette) ● ▣

  Familiar Mother Goose rhymes are chanted and sung to music with appropriate narration for young children.   *(1–5)*

- Wright, Blanche Fisher. **Real Mother Goose.** Special anniversary ed. Rand McNally 1916. 128p col illus.

  The checkerboard cover and the old-fashioned illustrations have kept this collection of over seventy rhymes popular for more than seventy years. *(0–3)*

- Yolen, Jane, editor. **The Lullaby Songbook.** Musical arrangements by Adam Stemple. Illus. by Charles Mikolaycak. Harcourt 1986. 31p col illus.

  Richly colored borders and illustrations frame a selection of fifteen lullabies, some of them treasured, a few of them less familiar. Music for piano and guitar as well as notes about the origin of each song are included. *(0–5)*

- Zemach, Margot. **Hush Little Baby.** Dutton (p) 1987. unpaged col illus.

  A wailing baby is promised a series of gifts, which are portrayed in hilarious, wacky illustrations. The music for the melody is included. *(1–5)*

Folktales

Folktales convey values that transcend time and cultural boundaries. Each year numerous retellings and newly illustrated versions of these old familiar stories are published. The tales endure not because of their pictures, but because of their universal themes and their language.

The versions recommended here have simple plots and sometimes include refrains young children enjoy repeating. Folktales come from an oral tradition. Feel free to retell them yourself and encourage your audience to join in.

- Aardema, Verna. **Who's in Rabbit's House?** Illus. by Leo and Diane Dillon. Dial (h&p) 1977. unpaged col illus.

  All the animals suggest ways for Rabbit to drive the Long One out of his house, but none succeed until they employ Frog's scheme, which finally frightens the caterpillar and drives him out. (3–5)

- Aardema, Verna. **Bringing the Rain to Kapiti Plain: A Nandi Tale.** Illus. by Beatriz Vidal. Dial (h&p) 1981. unpaged col illus.

  The story of the parched plains of Kapiti and of the boy Ki-Pat, who finds a way to release the rain from the dark, full clouds, is told in rhythmic, cumulative verse. Drawings of native African animals illustrate the text. (4–5)

- Bang, Molly. **The Paper Crane.** Greenwillow 1985. unpaged col illus.

  In exchange for his dinner, a poor stranger gives the restaurant owner a paper crane, which, at the clap of hands, comes to life and dances. News of the magical crane brings fame and prosperity to the restaurant. The intricate paper collages create elegant, three-dimensional pictures with a Japanese style. (3–5)

  A read-along cassette is available from Random House. ●●

- Bennett, Jill. **Teeny Tiny.** Illus. by Tomie dePaola. Putnam 1985. unpaged col illus.

  A slightly scary, fun story about the teeny tiny woman who finds a teeny tiny bone in a churchyard and takes it home to make soup . . . but the bone is eerily reclaimed. (3–5)

• Brett, Jan. **Goldilocks and the Three Bears.** Dodd, Mead 1987. unpaged col illus.

The classic story is retold with fascinating, detailed illustrations of the bears' woodsy home.   *(4–5)*

• Brown, Marcia. **Stone Soup.** Macmillan/Aladdin (p) 1947. unpaged 2-col illus.

Three clever soldiers make stone soup for the village people, who unwittingly provide the ingredients for a feast.   *(3–5)*

• Bryan, Ashley. **The Cat's Purr.** Atheneum 1985. 42p b&w illus.

Rat plays a trick on his friend Cat and takes Cat's family drum. Cat almost eats Rat but swallows the small drum instead. Since then the purring—purrum, purrum, purrum—of the drum can be heard whenever Cat is gently stroked.   *(2–5)*

A read-along cassette is available from Random House. ▪▪

• Castle, Caroline. **The Hare and the Tortoise.** Illus. by Peter Weevers. Dial (h&p) 1985. Unpaged col illus.

This is an adaptation of the well-known fable from Aesop about the race between the arrogant Hare and the slow-moving Tortoise, with full-page watercolor paintings and smaller sepia sketches.   *(1–5)*

• Cook, Scott. **The Gingerbread Boy.** Knopf 1987. unpaged col illus.

"You can't catch me, I'm the Gingerbread Man!" a plump gingerbread boy calls in succession to a little old woman and man, a cow, a horse, threshers, and mowers until finally a sly fox outsmarts him and gobbles him up. Cinnamon-toned illustrations are a delicious accompaniment to the familiar story.   *(0–5)*

• Emberley, Barbara, adapter. **Drummer Hoff.** Illus. by Ed Emberley. Prentice-Hall (h&p) 1967. unpaged col illus.

The general, major, captain, sergeant, corporal, and private each have a special role in preparing and loading a cannon. Children love the cumulative rhyming verse and the final Kahbahbloom when Drummer Hoff fires it off. (1–5)

• Galdone, Paul. **Henny Penny.** Clarion (h&p) 1968. unpaged col illus.

This retelling of the familiar tale of Henny Penny, who tells everyone the sky is falling, includes a surprise ending. (0–5)

A read-along kit is available from Spoken Arts. ●●

• Galdone, Paul. **The Three Billy Goats Gruff.** Clarion 1973. unpaged col illus.

A terrible troll lives under a bridge which three goats must cross. The first two tell the troll he should wait to eat the next goat, who is much bigger. The troll meets his match when the last and biggest goat crosses the bridge. (2–5)

• Grant, Joan. **The Monster That Grew Small: An Egyptian Folktale.** Illus. by Jill Karla Schwarz. Lothrop 1987. unpaged col illus.

Miobi, a timid young boy, befriends a hare despite his own fears. In return, the hare tells him where he can find courage. Miobi saves a village from a monster that grows larger when he runs from it in fear but becomes smaller as he overcomes his fear and runs toward it. This appeals to a small child's fascination with monsters and has a comforting resolution. (5)

- Hogrogian, Nonny. **One Fine Day.** Macmillan (h&p) 1971. unpaged col illus.

  A fox drinks the milk from an old woman's pail. She cuts off his tail and then won't sew it back on until he replaces her milk. This crisp retelling of the familiar chain story features lustrous full-page illustrations. *(3–5)*

- Jacobs, Joseph. **Jack and the Beanstalk.** Retold and illus. by Lorinda Bryan Cauley. Putnam (h&p) 1983. unpaged col illus.

  Jack swaps his mother's cow for a handful of beans, climbs the beanstalk, and must escape from a fearsome giant before acquiring the giant's great wealth. Retold with rich, full-page oil paintings. *(3–5)*

- Jacobs, Joseph. **The Three Little Pigs.** Illus. by Erik Blegvad. Atheneum 1980. 31p col illus.

  Delightful, detailed color-pencil and pen-and-ink illustrations fill this small book. The pigs, two dressed in knickers and one in a natty suit, have real character, and the wolf leers appropriately. *(0–5)*

- La Fontaine, Jean. **The Lion and the Rat.** Illus. by Brian Wildsmith. Oxford (h&p) 1963. unpaged col illus.

  The familiar fable about a rat who was able to rescue a lion is here retold with bright, appealing illustrations. *(3–5)*

- La Fontaine, Jean. **The Miller, the Boy and the Donkey.** Retold and illus. by Brian Wildsmith. Oxford (h&p) 1969. unpaged col illus.

  A miller tries carrying, riding, and walking a donkey to market and finds that no matter what he does, he can't please everyone. Finally he decides to please himself. *(2–5)*

- Lobel, Arnold. **Ming Lo Moves the Mountain.** Greenwillow (h) Scholastic (p). 1982, 32p col illus.

Full-page watercolor illustrations reminiscent of Chinese paintings depict the story of Ming Lo and his wife, who try to move the mountain that towers over their home. Their problem is humorously resolved.

(2–5)

A read-along kit is available from Scholastic. ●●

- Marshall, James. **Red Riding Hood.** Dial 1987. unpaged col illus.

A lighthearted retelling of the classic tale, with bright and lively illustrations. This is less threatening than other versions and has more appeal for younger children. *(2–5)*

- Sawyer, Ruth. **Journey Cake, Ho!** Illus. by Robert McCloskey. Viking (h) Puffin (p) 1953. 45p 2-color illus.

Johnny is joined in his pursuit of the journey cake by several barnyard animals in this rollicking tale. *(2–5)*

- Turkle, Brinton. **Deep in the Forest.** Dutton (p) 1976. unpaged 2-color illus.

A young bear enters a house in the woods, samples the porridge, sits in all the chairs, and lies in all of the beds. A delightful twist on the familiar and beloved "Three Bears," told entirely without words.

(2–5)

- Zemach, Margot. **Little Red Hen: An Old Story.** Penguin (p) 1987. unpaged col illus.

A crisp retelling of the story of the hardworking hen and her lazy friends, with delightful illustrations. *(0–5)*

Contemporary Classics

Nursery rhymes and folklore form the pool of traditional classics for young children. Books published in this century achieve "classic" designation when they continually appeal to succeeding generations of young listeners.

Format and design have changed over the past ninety years. Brightly colored illustrations and large, clear type predominate today. Many of the old favorites, with their black-and-white illustrations and smaller type, appear to fall short. They don't. Their timeless language, characters, and storylines hit a virtually universal responsive chord. Happily too, these titles are easy to locate on the shelves of bookstores and libraries because of their enduring popularity.

• Bemelmans, Ludwig. **Madeline.** Viking (h) Puffin (p) 1962. unpaged col illus.

The littlest girl in a boarding school in Paris is forever getting into scrapes. The cadence and rhyme of the text and the vivacity of the illustrations have made **Madeline** *and its sequels enduringly popular.*

(2–5)

A book and cassette read-along kit is available from Live Oak Media. Carol Channing on the record/cassette **Madeline and Other Bemelmans** *(Harper Audio) reads the stories with flair.* ◐ ▥

• Bright, Robert. **Georgie.** Doubleday (h) Scholastic (p) 1944. unpaged illus.

Feeling unwanted, Georgie, an endearing ghost, decides to leave home when the Whitakers nail down the step he's been creaking. This highly popular series includes, among other titles, **Georgie and the Robbers; Georgie and the Magician;** *and* **Georgie's Christmas Carol.** *(2–5)*

• Bright, Robert. **My Red Umbrella.** Morrow 1959. unpaged col illus.

Growing larger, to accommodate one animal after another, a small girl's umbrella provides shelter from the rain in this small, pleasing book. *(2–5)*

• Brown, Margaret Wise. **Goodnight Moon.** Pictures by Clement Hurd. Harper & Row (h&p) 1949. unpaged col illus.

As the illustrations change from bright to soft, dark colors, a little bunny says goodnight to each of the familiar things of his world. Children inevitably trace the changing position of the young mouse.

(0–5)

A read-along kit is available from Live Oak Media. ▥

- Burton, Virginia Lee. **Mike Mulligan and His Steam Shovel.** Houghton Mifflin (h&p) 1939. unpaged col illus.

  Although steam shovels are rapidly being replaced by newer machines, Mike Mulligan and his steam shovel Mary Anne prove their worth to the town of Popperville. (2–5)

  A read-along kit is available from Houghton Mifflin. ▨

  Other popular stories by the author are **Katy and the Big Snow; Choo, Choo;** *and* **The Little House.**

- de Brunhoff, Jean. **The Story of Babar, the Little Elephant.** Translated from the French by Merle S. Haas. Random House 1933. 47p col illus.

  After his mother has been shot by a hunter, a little elephant runs away from the jungle and goes to Paris, where he lives with a kind old lady and acquires clothing and schooling but soon grows homesick. (2–5)

  A record/cassette narrated by Peter Ustinov is available from Angel Records, 1966. ●▨

- Duvoisin, Roger. **Petunia.** Knopf 1950. unpaged col illus.

  The ultimate silly goose, Petunia thinks she will become wise by carrying a book around under her wing. (3–5)

  Some of the other episodes about this dimwitted but lovable fowl are recounted in **Petunia, I Love You** *and* **Petunia, Beware.** *Six of her adventures are read by Julie Harris on* **Petunia** *(Harper Audio).* ▨

- Eastman, P. D. **Are You My Mother?** Random House (h&p) 1960. 63p col illus.

  Very simple vocabulary and cartoonlike illustrations follow a baby bird's search for his mother. Youngsters soon memorize the text of this one and "read" it themselves. (2–5)

Go, Dog. Go! and **Sam and the Firefly** are also popular books by this author.

Read-along kits are available from Random House for **Are You My Mother?** and **Go, Dog. Go!** ◘◘

- Ets, Marie Hall. **In the Forest.** Penguin (p) 1944. unpaged b&w illus.

Several animals form a parade behind a small boy, who is wearing a paper hat and blowing a horn as they walk through the forest. (1–5)

A read-along kit is available from Live Oak Media. ◘◘

- Fatio, Louise. **The Happy Lion.** Illus. by Roger Duvoisin. Mc-Graw-Hill (h) Scholastic (p) 1964. unpaged col and b&w illus.

Venturing out from his home in a zoo in France to visit friends, the happy lion causes considerable consternation until he gets back home again with the help of a young friend. The benign nature of the beast usually thought of as fierce has made this and other titles in the series enduring favorites. (2–5)

- Flack, Marjorie. **Angus and the Ducks.** Puffin (p) 1933. unpaged col illus.

Angus, a Scottie pup, is curious about everything, especially the ducks in the next garden. But he runs into trouble when he finally encounters them. (1–5)

His curiosity leads to further adventures in **Angus and the Cat.**

- Flack, Marjorie, and Kurt Wiese. **The Story About Ping.** Viking (h) Puffin (p) 1933. 32p col illus.

  Knowing that he'll be spanked for being the last duck to get back on board the houseboat, Ping tries to evade his fate, only to find himself in greater danger.   *(2–5)*

  A read-along kit is available from Live Oak Media. ●●

- Freeman, Don. **Corduroy.** Viking (h) Puffin (p) 1968. 32p col illus.

  Saddened when a little girl's mother says she can't buy him because of a missing button, Corduroy, a stuffed bear, sets out to remedy the situation.   *(3–5)*

  In **A Pocket for Corduroy** *Corduroy gets locked up in a laundromat overnight.*

  Read-along kits are available from Live Oak Media. ●●

  Freeman's other books, including **Norman the Doorman, Pet of the Met,** *and* **Guard Mouse,** *are popular with slightly older children.*

- Gág, Wanda. **The A B C Bunny.** Hand-lettered by Howard Gág. Coward McCann (h) Putnam (p) 1933. unpaged 2-col illus.

  A bouncy, memorable rhyme leads the reader from A to "Z is for zero—close the book." Words and music for the song are included. A beloved classic, deservedly so.   *(1–3)*

- Gág, Wanda. **Millions of Cats.** Coward McCann (h&p) 1928. unpaged b&w illus.

  In search of one cat, a very old man and woman find themselves overrun with "millions and billions and trillions" of cats. Young children join in on the refrain.   *(2–5)*

- Gramatky, Hardie. **Little Toot.** Putnam (h&p) 1939. unpaged col illus.

  Chided by his elders and betters for his constant playfulness, Little Toot, the tugboat, proves his mettle when he helps a large ocean liner in distress. (2–5)

- Hutchins, Pat. **Rosie's Walk.** Macmillan (h&p) 1968. unpaged col illus.

  A hen goes for a walk, oblivious to the fact that she's being stalked by a fox. The very simple text, the double-page illustrations, and the predictability of the calamities that occur to the fox have made this eminently appealing. (1–5)

- Krauss, Ruth. **The Carrot Seed.** Illus. by Crockett Johnson. Harper 1945. unpaged col illus.

  Everyone says it won't grow, but a little boy carefully tends the seed he has planted until he eventually proves them wrong. (2–5)

- Krauss, Ruth. **A Hole Is to Dig.** Illus. by Maurice Sendak. Harper 1952. unpaged b&w illus.

  Black-line drawings interpret childlike definitions of what certain things—a hole, a hat, the world—are for. (4–5)

- Leaf, Munro. **The Story of Ferdinand.** Illus. by Robert Lawson. Viking (h) Puffin (p) 1936. unpaged illus.

  Appearances can be deceiving. The young muscular bull, Ferdinand, would rather sit and smell the flowers than fight in the bull ring. (2–5)

  A read-along kit is available from Live Oak Media. ▧

- Lionni, Leo. **Swimmy.** Pantheon (h) Knopf (p) 1963. unpaged col illus.

  A small fish manages to protect the other fish in his school in an ingenious manner. The oversized pictures that illustrate the text are absorbing in their beauty. (2–5)

  A read-along kit is available from Random House. ▣

  Four beloved Lionni paperbacks, **Frederick, Swimmy, Alexander and the Wind-Up Mouse,** *and* **Fish Is Fish** *are packaged with a read-along cassette in* **Frederick and His Friends** *(Knopf).* ▣

- McCloskey, Robert. **Blueberries for Sal.** Viking (h) Puffin (p) 1948. 54p col illus.

  A little girl and her mother pick blueberries on one side of the hill while a bear cub and his mother are busy eating blueberries on the other side. The youngsters manage to get separated from their respective parents, and a surprise ensues. (2–5)

  A read-along kit is available from Live Oak Media. ▣

- McCloskey, Robert. **Make Way for Ducklings.** Viking (h) Puffin (p) 1963. unpaged b&w illus.

  Mr. and Mrs. Mallard set out to raise a family of ducklings in the middle of Boston. The detailed illustrations add to the charm of the story. (1–5)

  A read-along kit is available from Live Oak Media. ▣

- McCloskey, Robert. **Time of Wonder.** Viking (h) Penguin (p) 1957. 63p col illus.

  A soft, quietly poetic text and beautiful illustrations describe a family on an island in Maine as they experience a summer hurricane. (3–5)

- Milne, A. A. **Winnie-the-Pooh.** With decorations by Ernest H. Shepard. Dutton (h) 1926 Dell (p). 161p b&w illus.

  The adventures of the entirely lovable bear "with very little brain" and his friends Christopher Robin, Rabbit, Piglet, Eeyore, Kanga, and Roo delight reader and listener equally, though at very different levels. **The House at Pooh Corner** *contains further episodes. The two titles are available in a larger combined volume,* **The World of Pooh.**   (3–5)

  The reading by Maurice Evans (available both as a record and as a cassette) contains the right amount of dry humor and subtle matter-of-factness (Pathways of Sound). ⊙ ▣

  Carol Channing's readings from **The House at Pooh Corner**— *"Winnie-the-Pooh and Tigger," "Winnie-the-Pooh and Kanga and Roo," "Winnie-the-Pooh and Christopher Robin," and "Winnie-the-Pooh and Eeyore"—are more stylized but are still appealing (Harper Audio).* ▣

- Milne, A. A. **The World of Christopher Robin, The Complete When We Were Very Young and Now We are Six.** New illus. in full color by Ernest H. Shepard. Dutton 1958. 234p col illus.

  Verses—witty, whimsical or contemplative in nature—have become landmarks of childhood. From "Buckingham Palace" to "Disobedience" to "The King's Breakfast," the images and cadence have stimulated appreciation of language.   (2–5)

  Choice records/cassettes are available from Harper Audio. Dame Judith Anderson, the noted actress, reads selections from the two volumes of verse on **When We Were Very Young** *in an elegant style, while Carol Channing sings* **The Pooh Songbook** *in a sprightly manner.* ▣

- Minarik, Else Holmeland. **Little Bear.** Pictures by Maurice Sendak. Harper (h&p) 1961. 63p col illus.

  Four stories about Little Bear, who gets dressed, has a birthday, goes to the moon, and makes a wish. The simple text, gentle humor, and episodic format have made Little Bear and its companions— **Father**

Bear Comes Home, Little Bear's Visit, *and* **A Kiss for Little Bear**—*popular.* (2–5)

Read-along kits are available from Harper for **Little Bear, Little Bear's Friend,** *and* **Little Bear's Visit.** 🔲

- Piper, Watty, reteller. **The Little Engine That Could,** the complete, original edition. Illus. by George and Doris Hauman. Platt & Munk (h) Putnam (p) 1930. unpaged col illus.

The train that carries good things for children is unable to go over the mountain until a small engine offers to help. The refrain, "I think I can, I think I can," is chanted with enthusiasm. (3–5)

A read-along kit is available from Listening Library. 🔲

- Potter, Beatrix. **The Tailor of Gloucester.** Warne 1931. 58p col illus.

A poor tailor taken ill just before being able to finish a wedding suit is helped by mice on Christmas Eve. The illustrations and the text combine to make a truly heartwarming story. (3–5)

- Potter, Beatrix. **The Tale of Peter Rabbit.** Warne (h&p). 58p col illus.

Disobeying his mother's instructions and going into Mr. McGregor's garden, Peter loses his way, is chased, and is trapped in a watering can for several hours before effecting his escape. The small size of the book, the charm of the pastel-hued watercolor paintings, and the integrity of the text ensure appeal. (2–5)

The companion tales, among them **The Tale of Mr. Jeremy Fisher, The Tale of Benjamin Bunny, The Tale of Mrs. Tiggy-Winkle, The Tale of Squirrel Nutkin,** *are also constant favorites.*

The record/cassettes **The Tale of Peter Rabbit and Four Other**

Stories, The Tale of the Flopsy Bunnies and Five Other Stories, and The Tale of Squirrel Nutkin and Three Other Stories, *read expressively by Claire Bloom on the Harper Audio label, are superior.* ○ ▯▯

- Rey, H. A. **Curious George.** Houghton Mifflin (h&p) 1941. 56p col illus.

  The irrepressible little monkey manages to get into a series of mischievous scrapes that provoke grins, giggles, and shouts of laughter from young listeners. (1–5)

  Julie Harris reads **Curious George and Other Tales About Curious George** *(available both as a record and as a cassette) with appeal and aplomb on the Harper Audio label.* ○ ▯▯

- Sandburg, Carl. **The Wedding Procession of the Rag Doll and the Broom Handle and Who Was in It.** Pictures by Harriet Pincus. Harcourt (h&p) 1950. unpaged col illus.

  The rib-tickling style of **Rootabaga Stories** *is exemplified by the story of the wedding of the Rag Doll and Broom Handle and the many wedding guests, including the Spoon Lickers, the Tin Pan Bangers, the Chocolate Chins, the Dirty Bibs, the Clean Ears, and the Easy Ticklers.* (1–5)

- Sendak, Maurice. **The Nutshell Library.** Harper 1962. unpaged col illus.

  These four small books fit nicely into the hand. Zestful illustrations and perky text feature the alphabet, in **Alligators All Around;** *counting, in* **One Was Johnny;** *the calendar, in* **Chicken Soup with Rice;** *and the adventures of a boy who always said, "I don't care," in* **Pierre.** (1–5)

- Sendak, Maurice. **Where the Wild Things Are.** Harper (h&p) 1963. unpaged col illus.

Sent to his room without any supper for behaving outrageously, Max imagines a voyage to the land of the wild things where a glorious rumpus ensues. Despite the excitement, Max finds that he'd rather be "where someone loves him best of all," and goes home to find "his supper waiting for him and it was still hot." Despite the feelings of many adults that the wild things would frighten youngsters, the vast majority of children have taken the creatures to their hearts. **Where the Wild Things Are** *is a superb confirmation of love.*   (1–5)

The record and cassette available from Harper Audio and read effectively by Tammy Grimes features the text of **Where the Wild Things Are** *and the stories in* **The Nutshell Library,** *among others.* ○ ▭

- Seuss, Dr. **And to Think That I Saw It on Mulberry Street.** Random House 1937. unpaged col illus.

On his return from school, a boy recounts the fantastic sights his imagination developed, from the horse and cart he saw to a circus bandwagon drawn by an elephant and two giraffes. The simple drawings reflect the wit of the text.   (2–5)

Dr. Seuss's second book, **The Five Hundred Hats of Bartholomew Cubbins,** *delights readers with its fantastic humor and dramatic tension.* **Horton Hatches the Egg** *and* **How the Grinch Stole Christmas** *are also very popular.*

In addition, with **The Cat in the Hat, Green Eggs and Ham, Hop on Pop,** *and* **Fox in Socks,** *he launched the entire genre of creative controlled-vocabulary books for beginning readers. Dr. Seuss has made a truly lasting contribution to children's literature.*

Hans Conried's witty reading of **Happy Birthday to You and Other Stories** *(Harper Audio, available as a record and as a cassette), augmented with sound effects, is a fine complement to the books.* ○ ▭

• Slobodkina, Esphyr. **Caps for Sale: A Tale of a Peddler, Some Monkeys & Their Monkey Business.** Harper (h&p) 1947. unpaged col illus.

Napping under a tree with his caps stacked on his head, a peddler wakes to find them adorning monkeys who taunt him. He finally manages to retrieve the hats by making use of the monkeys' imitative behavior. (1–5)

A read-along kit is available from Live Oak Media.

• Taylor, Mark. **Henry the Explorer.** Illus. by Graham Booth. Little, Brown (p) 1966. unpaged col illus.

Henry and his dog, Angus, go exploring in the snow, leaving small flags to claim each of their discoveries. When they end up in a cave inhabited by bears, they decide it's time to go home—but which way? (3–5)

• Tresselt, Alvin. **Hide and Seek Fog.** Illus. by Roger Duvoisin. Lothrop 1965. unpaged col illus.

Fog settles on a seaside village and the inhabitants find ways to pass the time. Misty, foggy illustrations capture the serene mood. (3–5)

• Turkle, Brinton. **Thy Friend, Obadiah.** Viking (h) Puffin (p) 1969. unpaged col illus.

Obadiah is teased by his brothers and sister because a sea gull has adopted him as a friend and persists in following him everywhere. One day the bird doesn't appear, and Obadiah searches for him, realizing that he is the sea gull's friend too. Warm illustrations capture colonial life in the fishing village of Nantucket. (3–5)

In **Rachel and Obadiah,** *Rachel beats her older brother in a foot race because he stops to eat blackberries along the way.*

• Yashima, Taro. **Umbrella.** Viking (h) Puffin (p) 1958. 30p col illus.

Three-year-old Momo waits impatiently for rain so she can use her new red boots and umbrella. (2–5)

A read-along kit is available from Live Oak Media. ◘◘

Poetry

Rhythm and rhyme are the most commonly thought of characteristics of poetry. The former always exists but the latter is not required. An element less often mentioned is poetry's way of succinctly capturing the moment—whether the moment is an event, a thing, or, more subtly and elusively, a feeling.

Many adults who bear scars from high school and college English classes are intimidated by this form of literature. Poetry written or collected for children dispels all bad memories. It is, by and large, exuberant and vivacious and truly astonishing in its variety.

- Adoff, Arnold. **Black Is Brown Is Tan.** Illus. by Emily Arnold McCully. Harper 1973. 32p col illus.

  A warm celebration of family and race in free verse and colorful illustrations. Features a loving biracial family: "There is granny white and grandma black/kissing both your cheeks and hugging back." (2–5)

- Blishen, Edward, compiler. **The Oxford Book of Poetry for Children.** Illus. by Brian Wildsmith. Oxford (h&p) 1963. 168p col illus.

  Classic and popular English poets are featured in this collection, which has the added benefit of Brian Wildsmith's brightly colored and angular paintings. (0–5)

- Bober, Natalie S. **Let's Pretend.** Illus. by Bill Bell. Viking/Kestrel 1986. 68p col illus.

  A compilation from various poets, including Shel Silverstein, Emily Dickinson, Rose Fyleman, and Robert Louis Stevenson, emphasizing the imaginative world of children. Colored illustrations are very stylized, almost cartoonish, in their portrayal of the land of make-believe. While there are not many illustrations, the language of the poems creates vibrant images. (4–5)

- Chorao, Kay. **The Baby's Good Morning Book.** Dutton 1986. 64p col illus.

  Nursery rhymes and poems by such well-known writers as Browning, Wordsworth, and Dickinson are interpreted in brightly colored and detailed watercolor and pen-and-ink pictures. (2–4)

- Clifton, Lucille. **Some of the Days of Everett Anderson.** Illus. by Evaline Ness. Henry Holt 1970. unpaged 2-col illus.

  Lively poems highlight the days in a week for Everett Anderson, who is

*six and black, and who lives in the city. Marvelous illustrations include
some double-page spreads.* (2–5)

- Cole, Joanna. **A New Treasury of Children's Poetry.** Illus. by
Judith Gwyn Brown. Doubleday 1984. 224p b&w illus.

*Mixing styles and subjects, this collection of over two hundred poems
by renowned authors is a comprehensive family anthology.* (1–5)

- Cummings, E. E. **In Just-Spring.** Illus. by Heidi Goennel. Little,
Brown 1988. unpaged col illus.

*A favorite poem to celebrate the new season, aptly illustrated with
bright colors and minimal details.* (3–5)

- Degen, Bruce. **Jamberry.** Harper (h&p) 1983. unpaged col illus.

*That all kinds of berries can be made into jam is clearly shown in
rhyming verse and bright, active paintings of a bear and a boy who love
them both.* (3–5)

A read-along kit is available from Live Oak Media.

- De Regniers, Beatrice Schenk, Eva Moore, Mary Michaels White,
and Jan Carr, editors. **Sing a Song of Popcorn.** Illus. by Marcia
Brown, Leo and Diane Dillon, Richard Egielski, Trina Schart
Hyman, Arnold Lobel, Maurice Sendak, Marc Simont, and
Margot Zemach. Scholastic 1988. 142p col illus.

*Don't be put off by the length of the bibliographic information. This
extensive and joyful anthology of well-known, appealing poems is
additionally noteworthy on two accounts: layout and illustrations. The
poems, generously surrounded by white space, are grouped by themes:
Mostly Weather, Spooky Poems, Mostly Animals, Mostly Nonsense,
Seeing, Feeling, Thinking. Each section is illustrated by a different
Caldecott Medal–winning artist. An instant classic.* (0–5)

• Frost, Robert. **Stopping by Woods on a Snowy Evening.** Illus. by Susan Jeffers. Dutton (h&p) 1978. unpaged col illus.

Soft pencil and watercolor double-page illustrations hint at a Christmas Eve setting, since the plump man driving the sleigh bears a certain resemblance to Santa Claus.   *(3–5)*

• Hoban, Russell. **Egg Thoughts and Other Frances Songs.** Illus. by Lillian Hoban. Harper 1972. 31p 2-color illus.

Lorna Doone cookies, friendship, and pets are among the musings of Frances, the little girl badger. Young listeners identify with Frances' insightful truths.   *(2–5)*

• Hopkins, Lee Bennett. **More Surprises.** Illus. by Megan Lloyd. Harper 1987. 64p col illus.

People, body parts, living things, hot and cold, and school are among the headings under which poems are placed. Large type and brightly colored illustrations make this an easy choice for sharing.   *(3–5)*

• Hughes, Shirley. **Out and About.** Lothrop 1988. unpaged col illus.

Mud, backyard swimming pools, the seaside, sick in bed, and Christmas are among the year-round concerns of children celebrated in rhyme and numerous warm illustrations.   *(2–5)*

• Krauss, Ruth. **I'll Be You and You Be Me.** Illus. by Maurice Sendak. Harper 1954. unpaged b&w illus.

Childlike poems and charming pen-and-ink sketches illuminate the innermost thoughts of many children.   *(3–5)*

- Lalicki, Barbara. **If There Were Dreams to Sell.** Illus. by Margot Tomes. Lothrop 1984. unpaged col illus.

  Each letter of the alphabet—shown in both upper and lower case—is paired with a rhyme, a poem or part of a poem, and/or an illustration. "Q" and "R" feature the rhyme "Queen of Hearts" fully illustrated with a recipe for raspberry tarts. Fanciful, droll illustrations pull together the compilation. (3–5)

- Lear, Edward. **The Owl and the Pussycat.** Illus. by Paul Galdone. Clarion 1987. unpaged col illus.

  Brightly colored double-page illustrations enliven and enlarge upon the nonsensical courtship and marriage of the unusual couple. (2–5)

- Livingston, Myra Cohn. **A Song I Sang to You.** Illus. by Margot Tomes. Harcourt 1984. unpaged b&w illus.

  From the lively—fits of laughter to the more pensive—thoughts about seasons—these short poems celebrate commonplace life. (4–5)

- Lobel, Arnold. **Whiskers and Rhymes.** Greenwillow 1985. 48p col illus.

  Original nursery rhymes, many direct takeoffs on Mother Goose rhymes, are humorously illustrated, entirely with felines. (2–5)

- McCord, David. **All Small.** Illus. by Madelaine Gill Linden. Little, Brown 1986. 32p col illus.

  Selected from the author's various other collections, these short poems are illustrated with dainty color illustrations. McCord is super! (3–5)

- Merriam, Eve. **Blackberry Ink.** Illus. by Hans Wilhelm. Morrow 1985. 40p col illus.

  Chant them, clap them out, these joyous and effervescent poems encourage an interest in poetry. (3–5)

• Merriam, Eve. **Out Loud: Playful Sound Poems.** Harper Audio 1988. (Cassette) ▇

The author reads several of her poems in an expressive voice with music and sound effects. (3–5)

• Pomerantz, Charlotte. **The Tamarindo Puppy and Other Poems.** Illus. by Byron Barton. Greenwillow 1980. 31p col illus.

The reader and listener feel the warm, gentle winds and the bright sunshine of the Caribbean as well as empathy for the homesick child narrator. The integration of some simple Spanish vocabulary is a plus, as are the bold and colorful illustrations. (3–5)

• Prelutsky, Jack. **Ride a Purple Pelican.** Illus. by Garth Williams. Greenwillow 1986. 64p col illus.

Large, boldly colored illustrations accompany nonsense verse. (2–5)

• Prelutsky, Jack, editor. **The Random House Book of Poetry for Children.** Illus. by Arnold Lobel. Random House 1983. 248p col illus.

Charming, witty illustrations enhance over 500 poems arranged in thematic sections. A visual and read-aloud delight. (0–5)

• Prelutsky, Jack, editor. **Read-Aloud Rhymes for the Very Young.** Illus. by Marc Brown. Knopf 1986. 98p col illus.

A bounty of rhymes for reading, whispering, and shouting out loud, with numerous humorous illustrations. (2–5)

A cassette and book are available in a kit from Random House. Cassette can be used alone or with the book. ▇

• Royds, Caroline, compiler. **Poems for Young Children.** Illus. by Inga Moore. Doubleday 1986. 64p col illus.

A collection of classic children's poems pleasingly illustrated with bright colors. (2–5)

- Silverstein, Shel. **Where the Sidewalk Ends.** Harper 1974. 166p b&w illus.

  Sardonic humor that neatly captures children's thoughts about the world is the keystone of these hilarious verses. Paired with the poet's lively ink drawings, they've come to be enjoyed by children and adults.   *(3–5)*

  A second collection, **A Light in the Attic,** *is just as appealing.*

  Cassettes recorded by the author from each title are available from Columbia. ▪▪

- Steele, Mary Q. **Anna's Summer Songs.** Pictures by Lena Anderson. Greenwillow 1988. 32p col illus.

  Irises, strawberries, oak trees, and honeysuckle are among the summer plants and flowers that are the subjects of the poems in this slender collection. A lovely way to view the season and its plants.   *(3–5)*

- Stevenson, Robert Louis. **A Child's Garden of Verses.**

  Relating common experiences of childhood, Stevenson's poems have maintained their child appeal for a century. Three editions, each appealing for unique reasons, are: the classic with old-fashioned illustrations by Jessie Wilcox Smith (Scribner's 1905); one with jewel-toned and vivacious illustrations of Brian Wildsmith (Oxford 1976); and an edition with fresh watercolor illustrations by Michael Foreman (Delacorte 1985).   *(0–5)*

- Stevenson, Robert Louis. **The Land of Nod and Other Poems for Children.** Selected and illustrated by Michael Hague. Henry Holt 1988. 51p col illus.

  A selection of 30 of Stevenson's poems, each with illustrations that capture the everyday and fantasy worlds of childhood.   *(2–5)*

- Untermeyer, Louis, editor. **Rainbow in the Sky.** Illus. by Reginald Birch. Harcourt 1935. 498p illus.

  This substantial anthology includes timeless classics. The format dictates it be used as a read-aloud resource for the entire family. (1–5)

- Zolotow, Charlotte. **Everything Glistens and Everything Sings.** Illus. by Margot Tomes. Harcourt 1987. 96p b&w illus.

  Small poems arranged by topics capture in words the sharp images of nature, friends, and family. (3–5)

Identification and Concept Books

Put yourself in the place of a very young child. Look at all the common, ordinary things you see, and imagine you've just started to realize there are sounds that are repeatedly associated with them. You don't understand quite that things have names, but you realize there is some kind of link between the things and the sounds.

Identification books help young children name animals, colors, sounds, articles of clothing, toys, etc. Concept books assist in their understanding of what is meant by the alphabet, numbers, spatial relationships, and so on. These books help them comprehend their everyday world. Many of these books are not exciting reading fare for adults, who prefer more extensive narrative, but most young children love them. What can be appreciated by both children and adults is the creativity that lies behind these very simple books.

- Ahlberg, Janet and Allan. **Baby's Catalogue.** Little, Brown (h&p) 1982. unpaged col illus.

  Six babies, their mothers and fathers, meals, baby furniture, toys, and activities are featured in humorous pictures to name and discuss. Babies will enjoy looking at other babies and thumbing through the "catalogue." Older children will enjoy talking about when they were babies or about their younger siblings. (0–3)

- Anno, Mitsumasa. **Anno's Counting Book.** Crowell (h) Harper (p) 1975. 28p col illus.

  The numbers 0 through 12 each have a double-page spread. Beginning with an empty landscape for zero, and then moving through the twelve months and the twelve hours as shown on a church clock, the landscape fills up with trees, houses, and people to count. A fine counting book and introduction to the uses of numbers. (2–5)

- Bang, Molly. **Ten, Nine, Eight.** Greenwillow (h) Puffin (p) 1983. unpaged col illus.

  A warm and loving countdown in soft rhyme and illustrations from ten washed toes to "Two strong arms around a fuzzy bear's head/One big girl all ready for bed." (0–5)

  Cassette available from Random House/Miller-Brody. ▣

- Berger, Terry. **Ben's ABC Day.** Photos by Alice S. Kandell. Lothrop 1982. 32p col photos.

  Ben's day begins upon "Awakening" and continues through 25 other familiar activities, one for each letter of the alphabet, shown in sharp color photographs. (2–5)

- Burningham, John. **John Burningham's ABC.** Crown 1986. unpaged col illus.

  Each letter of the alphabet is shown in upper and lower case with a familiar animal whose name starts with the appropriate letter in an uncluttered format. (2–5)

  In similar style and appeal are **John Burningham's 123** *and* **John Burningham's Colors.**

- Burningham, John. **Slam Bang.** Viking 1985. unpaged col illus.

  A young boy and his dog illustrate several noisy words while the dog drives them around in a convertible. Each page has one word humorously illustrated. Other books in this series of introductions to marvelously tactile words are: **Jangle Twang, Cluck Baa, Sniff Shout, Skip Trip,** *and* **Wobble Pop.** (1–3)

- Carle, Eric. **Let's Paint a Rainbow.** Philomel 1982. unpaged col illus.

  Cutout pages in this board book reveal painters adding different colors to one side of the page while mice are added to the opposite side, ending with a rainbow cat above four mice. (2–5)

- Charlip, Remy. **Handtalk: A Finger Spelling & Sign Language ABC.** By Remy Charlip, Mary Beth, and George Ancona. Parents Magazine Press (h) Four Winds/Macmillan (p) 1974. unpaged col illus.

  Expressive photographs demonstrate finger spelling and sign language. (5)

- Cleaver, Elizabeth. **ABC.** Atheneum 1984. unpaged col illus.

  On each left-hand page, one letter of the alphabet appears in upper and lower case and is followed by a short list of words beginning with that letter. The letter and objects named are combined in a colorful collage on the opposite page. Small size enhances the child appeal. (2–5)

- Domanska, Janina. **Busy Monday Morning.** Greenwillow, 1985. unpaged col illus.

  A Polish folk song about a boy and his father mowing, raking, drying, pitching, stacking, and hauling hay through the days of the week, and finally resting on Sunday. Attractive, brightly colored illustrations show father and son working together, while the simple repetitive text invites readers to sing along and to learn the days of the week. Includes musical notation. (1–5)

- Emberley, Ed. **Ed Emberley's ABC.** Illus. by Barbara and Michael Emberley. Little, Brown (h&p) 1978. unpaged col illus.

  A unique ABC book that not only features animals and objects beginning with each letter but imaginatively demonstrates how to construct each letter. (3–5)

- Giganti, Paul Jr. **How Many Snails.** Pictures by Donald Crews. Greenwillow 1988. unpaged col illus.

  An unpictured narrator observes clouds, flowers, fish, snails, starfish, dogs, books, and cupcakes. In each case the questions posed lead to increasing discrimination in counting and a beginning awareness of sets in mathematics. (3–5)

- Goor, Ron and Nancy. **Signs.** Crowell 1983. unpaged b&w photos.

  Stop, Exit, One Way, are among the familiar traffic and directional signs presented in handsomely composed photographs and minimal text. (2–5)

- Hoban, Tana. **Of Colors and Things.** Greenwillow 1989. unpaged col photos.

  Four photographs appear on each page. Photos of three brightly colored objects exemplify a particular hue while the fourth picture shows several different colors. The technical quality of the photographs is superb, and as usual, Hoban's wonderfully creative eye adds new dimensions to commonplace articles. (0–5)

- Hoban, Tana. **Red, Blue, Yellow Shoe.** Greenwillow 1986. unpaged col photos.

Red, blue, yellow, purple, orange, green, brown, gray, black, and white each have a page in this striking board book. The name of each color is accompanied by a crystal-clear photograph of a single object of that color. Other board books featuring the photographs of this artist are **Panda, Panda,** *in which a panda illustrates several activities;* **What Is It?,** *with photographs of some familiar objects; and* **1,2,3,** *a counting book.* (0–2)

- Hoban, Tana. **26 Letters and 99 Cents.** Greenwillow 1987. unpaged col photos.

A two-in-one book. Photographs of shiny plastic letters are paired with commonplace things that begin with the letter. After Z/zipper turn the book over and start counting through photographs of pennies, nickels, dimes, and quarters to see some of the different ways numbers can be put together. (2–5)

Hoban is the doyenne of artfully simple photographic identification and concept books. Among her many visually stunning books are **Is It Red? Is It Yellow? Is It Blue?,** *which focuses on colors;* **I Read Symbols,** *which addresses signs;* **Is It Rough? Is It Smooth? Is It Shiny?,** *which talks about textures; and* **Is It Larger? Is It Smaller?,** *which compares sizes.*

- Hughes, Shirley. **Bathwater's Hot.** Lothrop 1985. unpaged col illus.

A baby brother and older sister are featured along with family pets, toys, and other household clutter in this book about opposites. The Shirley Hughes Nursery Collection is an endearing series that also includes **When We Went to the Park,** *a counting book;* **Noisy,** *a book about sounds;* **All Shapes and Sizes; Colors;** *and* **Two Shoes, New Shoes,** *a book about clothing.* (1–3)

- Hutchins, Pat. **One Hunter.** Greenwillow (h) Mulberry (p) 1982. 24p col illus.

A hunter makes his determined way through a boldly colored jungle and is perplexed because he sees nothing to shoot—until he turns around and discovers he's followed by assorted animals. A counting book that is good for visual discrimination. (2–5)

- Isadora, Rachel. **I See.** Greenwillow 1985. unpaged col illus.

Attractive watercolor illustrations show a young toddler naming and responding to the various objects she sees in a day, from her teddy bear to her blocks to her crib. (0–2)

The same format is followed in **I Hear** *and* **I Touch.**

- Jenkins, Ella. **Counting Games and Rhythms for the Little Ones.** Vol. 1. Smithsonian Folkways, dist. by Rounder Records (Record).

Songs, rhymes, and games introduce concepts about numbers and counting. (2–5)

- Kightley, Rosalinda. **ABC.** Little, Brown 1986. unpaged col illus.

Each page in this bright attractive alphabet book shows the letter in upper and lower case, an appropriate object, and the name of the object spelled out at the bottom of the page in bold print.

- Kitchen, Bert. **Animal Alphabet.** Dial (h&p) 1984. unpaged col illus.

  Large, sophisticated drawings of animals, some quite unusual, illustrate each letter of the alphabet.   *(3–5)*

  Animal Numbers *highlights the numerals 1–10, 15, 25, 50, 75 and 100 and features the appropriate number of animal babies to count, and is equally attractive and appealing. A page of facts about the animals and their babies concludes the work.*

- Lionni, Leo. **What?** Pantheon 1983. unpaged col illus.

  A pair of animated cutout paper mice encounters a telephone, matches, glasses, a book, a ball, and cheese in this wordless board book, encouraging the reader to supply the words.   *(1–3)*

  Other titles in the series by the same author are **Who?**, **Where?**, *and* **When?**

- Lloyd, David. **Duck.** Illus. by Charlotte Voake. Lippincott 1988. unpaged col illus.

  Young Tim calls every animal he sees "duck," and every vehicle he sees "truck," until his grandmother shows him what a duck and truck really are. The watercolor sketches are just right for the loving tone of this book.   *(2–3)*

- Lobel, Arnold. **On Market Street.** Illus. by Anita Lobel. Greenwillow (h) Scholastic (p) 1981. unpaged col illus.

  Shop along Market Street and find items for the 26 letters of the alphabet. Each letter is imaginatively illustrated with a person composed entirely of different objects in a class of words beginning with that letter: For the letter V there is a person whose clothing and entire body—hair, face, arms, legs, and feet—are vegetables.   *(1–5)*

  Also available as a read-along cassette from Random House. ▮▮

- Lynn, Sara. **123.** Little, Brown 1986. unpaged col illus.

  A clean design, bold colors, and large type characterize this one-to-ten counting book. Each number features a numeral, the equivalent number of dots, the word for the number, and a bright picture of that number of farm animals. (2–5)

  Colors *introduces eleven familiar colors in a similar lucid format.*

- Maestro, Betsy and Giulio. **Camping Out: A Book of Action Words.** Crown 1985. 32p col illus.

  A man and an elephant demonstrate several active words involved in a camping trip. Similar treatment is given to clothing words in **On the Town** *and to pairs of opposites in* **Traffic.** (2–5)

- Maestro, Betsy and Giulio. **Where Is My Friend?** Crown (p) 1976. unpaged col illus.

  Searching for her friend, Harriet demonstrates directional and positional words such as up and down, around, under, and between. (2–5)

  Around the Clock with Harriet *goes through the hours of the day in a simple introduction to telling time.*

- Magee, Doug. **Trucks You Can Count On.** Dodd, Mead 1985. unpaged b&w photos.

  In a clever play on words, the title indicates the dual purpose of this book as a counting book and an introduction to the work done by trucks. Illustrated with clear black-and-white photographs of trucks and close-up parts of trucks. (3–5)

- McMillan, Bruce. **Becca Backward, Becca Frontward: A Book of Concept Pairs.** Lothrop 1986. unpaged col photos.

  Cheerful color photographs of four-year-old Becca illustrate several pairs of opposites. (1–5)

Here a Chick, There a Chick *follows a chick as it hatches from an egg and follows a trail of feed, demonstrating several pairs of directional opposites.*

Growing Colors *introduces colors from nature with stunning color photographs of fruits and vegetables and the plants they come from.*

- McNaught, Harry. **Words to Grow On.** Random House 1984. unpaged col illus.

Articles of furniture, clothing, utensils, and fixtures found throughout most homes are neatly identified in double-page illustrations.   (2–5)

- Morris, Ann. **Bread Bread Bread.** Photos by Ken Heyman. Lothrop 1989. 31p col photos.

Eaten all over the world, bread comes in many different forms, as shown by the colorful photographs and described in the very simple text. The index provides additional information about the pictured bread.

- Oxenbury, Helen. **Clap Hands.** Aladdin 1987. unpaged col illus.

*Larger in size than most board books, this features a different quartet of toddlers on each double-page spread. The rhyming, rhythmic phrases name common activities at day-care centers. Other titles in this Big Board Books series—***Tickle, Tickle; All Fall Down; Say Good-night***—take place in the same setting.*   (0–2)

- Oxenbury, Helen. **I Hear.** Random House 1986. unpaged col illus.

A familiar object is pictured alone and named on the left-hand page, while on the right-hand page a toddler is pictured doing something with the object.   (0–2)

The illustrations have a simple appeal in the Baby Board Books series, which also includes I Touch and I See. I Can varies the format with pictures of a toddler involved in a different familiar activity on each page.

- Pluckrose, Henry. **Knowabout Numbers.** Photos by Chris Fairclough. Watts 1988. unpaged col photos.

Bright photographs and simple text highlight the many uses of numbers in addresses, measurements, and sports. Photographs are predominantly European and some objects may require explanation, but the concepts are clear. (3–5)

- Pragoff, Fiona. **What Color? A Rainbow Zoo.** Doubleday 1987. unpaged col illus.

A striking introduction to colors, featuring brilliant photographs of animals on board pages with a spiral binding. (0–3)

The alphabet and numbers are featured in a similar format in **Alphabet** *and* **How Many: From Zero to Twenty. Growing: From First Cry to First Step** *traces infant development in delightful color photographs of babies. The very young enjoy the easy-to-turn pages and bright-colored photographs, and older children appreciate the concepts presented.*

- Reiss, John J. **Numbers.** Bradbury (h) Macmillan (p) 1971. unpaged col illus.

Numbers from one to one hundred are represented by brightly colored objects for counting. (3–5)

In **Shapes** *two- and three-dimensional shapes are introduced. These are somewhat sophisticated but exceptionally good examples of this genre.*

• Riddell, Edwina. **100 First Words to Say with Your Baby.** Barron's 1988. unpaged col illus.

Familiar scenes from a baby's life—the car, the grocery store, mealtime, and bath time—are depicted; the objects in the pictures are labeled for parents to point to and name for baby. (0–2)

• Rockwell, Anne. **In the Morning.** Crowell 1986. unpaged col illus.

A typical morning in the life of a young child is shown through an uncluttered format with brief text and simple illustrations. (0–2)

Other board books featuring familiar objects and activities beloved by young children are **At Night, At the Playground,** *and* **In the Rain.**

• Sawicki, Norma Jean. **The Little Red House.** Illus. by Tom Goffe. Lothrop 1989. unpaged col illus.

A young child lifts the roof of a little red house and finds nesting within it a smaller house of a different color. Each succeeding house yields yet another one until the final house gives up its surprise. (0–2)

• Schwartz, David M. **How Much Is a Million?** Illus. by Steven Kellogg. Lothrop (h) Scholastic (p) 1985. unpaged col illus.

Gain a sense of just how large a million, a billion and a trillion are through examples such as: How big a bowl would you need to hold a million goldfish? Whimsical illustrations and a note explaining the equations complete this unique work. (4–5)

- Serfozo, Mary. **Who Said Red?** Illus. by Keiko Narahasi. Atheneum/McElderry 1988. unpaged col illus.

  An exuberant introduction to the colors red, green, blue, and yellow as a young boy searches for his kite. (1–4)

- Spier, Peter. **Gobble Growl Grunt.** Doubleday 1971. unpaged col illus.

  Page after page is filled with all kinds of animals, clearly labeled with each animal's name and the sound it makes. A fun-filled, noisy book! (0–5)

  The companion title, **Crash Bang Boom,** *features household, machine, tool, and holiday sounds accompanied by detailed drawings.*

  In **Fast-Slow, High-Low** *basic concepts—including speed, number, size, and temperature—are introduced as pairs of opposites.*

- Tafuri, Nancy. **Two New Sneakers.** Greenwillow 1988. unpaged col illus.

  This board book features one brightly colored item of clothing on each page, all of which go on a small boy on the last page. (0–2)

  One Wet Jacket *gives similar treatment to a young girl's clothing.*

- Tafuri, Nancy. **Who's Counting?** Greenwillow 1986. unpaged col illus.

  Follow the puppy as he counts one squirrel, two birds, three moles, and on to a surprise at ten. Bold, striking double-page spreads are the real attraction of this successful counting book. (1–4)

- Testa, Fulvio. **If You Look Around You.** Dial (h&p) 1983. unpaged col illus.

  Meet and understand lines, dots, cylinders, spheres, and other geometric shapes in familiar childhood surroundings. (3–5)

- Trinca, Rod, and Kerry Argent. **One Woolly Wombat.** Kane-Miller (h&p) 1985. unpaged col illus.

  A counting book in rhyme vividly and humorously illustrated with Australian animals. (0–5)

Family

Parents, siblings, and sometimes grandparents are the people with whom young children spend most of their time. The family group establishes youngsters' sense of security. They use that support to venture forth, to test their physical environment, test behavior boundaries, and test relationships with family members.

Over the past twenty years the family has undergone significant demographic changes. There are more single-parent families. Divorce is no longer a rarity. More mothers work. Sometimes grandparents live far away, are younger, or are busy with their own activities.

Some things haven't changed. Even young children have to cope with life-cycle events—most commonly, the birth of a brother or sister. Older children are jealous of younger siblings. Younger siblings are anxious to be as independent as their older brothers and sisters.

Stories about family life echo these points. Whether the main characters are animal or human, the scenarios universally reflect both warmth and humor. Reassuring qualities, to be sure.

Parents

- Baum, Louis, **One More Time.** Illus. by Paddy Bouma. Morrow 1986. unpaged col illus.

  Simon and his dad sail their boat in the park, then gather their belongings and catch a train out of the city to Simon's mom, where Dad leaves him with a hug and "See you soon." Pleasant watercolor illustrations and the echoing dialogue between father and son express a warm and comfortable relationship between child and divorced parent.
  (2–5)

- Hazen, Barbara Shook. **Tight Times.** Illus. by Trina Schart Hyman. Viking (h) Puffin (p) 1979. unpaged b&w illus.

  Tight times are the reason a young boy's parents tell him he can't have a dog. When his father loses his job, it looks like times will get tighter. But when the boy brings home a stray kitten, his parents see beyond their problems and let him keep it. Black-and-white illustrations capture the difficult times and the family's emotions, enduring love, and respect for each other.
  (5)

- Himler, Ronald. **Wake Up, Jeremiah.** Harper 1979. unpaged col illus.

  Warm, impressionistic paintings and brief text portray a boy's rising and going out to meet the sunrise, then coming home to awaken his parents to the new day.
  (2–5)

- Hughes, Shirley. **Alfie Gets in First.** Lothrop (h) Mulberry (p) 1982. 32p col illus.

  Alfie runs home first and bangs the door shut. It locks, with his mother and baby sister on the outside. Clever illustrations show the activity on both sides of the door. Alfie is crying while his mother, the neighbors, the milkman, and the window cleaner all try to unlock the door. Finally Alfie gets a stool and proudly unlatches the door himself. (2–5)

In **Alfie's Feet** *Alfie gets new yellow boots and learns about left and right.* **Alfie Gives a Hand** *and* **Evening at Alfie's** *are two other equally delightful stories.*

• Johnson, Angela. **Tell Me a Story, Mama.** Illus. by David Soman. Orchard 1989. unpaged col illus.

A young African American girl's bedtime is made special by the stories she and her mother tell about the mother's girlhood. This can spark new tales for each family that reads it. (3–5)

• Kraus, Robert. **Whose Mouse Are You?** Pictures by Jose Aruego. Macmillan (h&p) 1970. unpaged col illus.

Nobody's mouse despairs because his mother is in the cat, his father is in a trap, his sister is lost, and he has no brother. A simple text presented in question-and-answer form and paired with large colorful illustrations has a happy resolution. (1–5)

• Lexau, Joan M. **Me Day.** Pictures by Robert Weaver. Dial 1971. unpaged b&w illus.

Rafer knows his birthday will be a special day with no chores and a birthday cake, but he particularly looks forward to receiving a letter from his father, since his parents are divorced. He is disappointed when he doesn't hear from his father but gets a wonderful surprise when his mother sends him on an errand. (4–5)

• Lobel, Arnold. **Mouse Tales.** Harper (h&p) 1972. 61p col illus.

Father Mouse tells each of his seven sons a nonsense bedtime story.
(3–5)

A read-along kit is available from Harper Audio. ◖◗

• Loh, Morag. **Tucking Mommy In.** Illus. by Donna Rawlins. Orchard 1988. unpaged col illus.

Mommy is so tired that she falls asleep putting her two daughters to bed. They sweetly wake her, lead her to her room, help her undress, and put her to bed with a kiss and a story. Soft, colorful illustrations portray the warm and peaceful family bedtime. (3–5)

• Long, Earlene. **Gone Fishing.** Illus. by Richard Brown. Houghton Mifflin 1984. 32p col illus.

Starting out early with "A big breakfast for my daddy. A little breakfast for me," a small boy and his father go fishing and catch a big and little fish for daddy and a little and big fish for the boy. A warm and loving portrayal of father and son in large pictures and simple text. (2–5)

• McCully, Emily Arnold. **Picnic.** Harper 1984. unpaged col illus.

Lively, colorful illustrations tell the wordless story of a large family of mice who go off in the truck for a picnic. Along the way, one small mouse falls out and is not missed until lunchtime, when they all go back to find her. (2–5)

• McPhail, David. **Emma's Pet.** Dutton 1985. unpaged col illus.

Finding the best pet isn't easy, and for one reason or another a bug, a bird, a frog, a snake, a mouse, a turtle, and a fish won't do until the younger bear girl finds the perfect cuddly pet where she least expected it. Warm watercolors enhance the story of a father and daughter's love. (2–5)

- McPhail, David. **Farm Morning.** Harcourt 1985. unpaged col illus.

  A little girl gets up early to help her father with the animals on their farm. Soft watercolor illustrations capture the morning light and the loving companionship of father and daughter. (2–5)

- Murphy, Jill. **Five Minutes' Peace.** Putnam 1986. unpaged col illus.

  Mrs. Large tries to get away from her three elephant children for "five minutes' peace from all of you" to take a bath, but one by one the three join her in the tub. Finally she escapes to the kitchen for "three minutes and forty-five seconds of peace." A familiar family scene amusingly illustrated with a family of elephants. (3–5)

  In **All in One Piece,** *Mr. and Mrs. Large's attempts to dress for an evening out are stymied by their dirty children.* **A Piece of Cake** *finds the entire family suffering when Mrs. Large decides to diet.*

- Ormerod, Jan. **Moonlight.** Lothrop (h) Puffin (p) 1982. unpaged col illus.

  The evening activities of a young girl are depicted entirely in pictures as she helps with the dishes, takes a bath, and gets ready for bed. She doesn't stay in bed but tries numerous stalls until her father ends up asleep in her bed and she and her mother end up asleep on the sofa. (2–5)

  The companion title **Sunshine** *depicts the family's morning routine.*

- Ormerod, Jan. **Making Friends.** Lothrop 1987. unpaged col illus.

  Baby and a black cat help Mom as she sews a simple doll for Baby to play with. **Mom's Home, Bend and Stretch,** *and* **This Little Nose** *also depict the threesome sharing simple activities and cuddles. Mom is expecting another baby, and the close spacing of her two children is somewhat atypical, but these are among the few books for very young children that feature a pregnant mother.* (1–2)

- Ormerod, Jan. **Sleeping.** Lothrop 1985. unpaged col illus.

  Dad's sleeping until his young toddler decides to climb up, bounce on the bed, and pull his nose. (0–3)

  More amusing and warm vignettes featuring Dad and the baby follow in **Dad's Back, Messy Baby,** *and* **Reading.**

- Rice, Eve. **Benny Bakes a Cake.** Greenwillow 1981. unpaged col illus.

  Benny helps his mother bake a birthday cake. They get ready to go for a walk and look for Ralph, the dog. They find him in the kitchen devouring the cake. Benny is inconsolable until his father comes home with another cake. (3–5)

- Rylant, Cynthia. **Birthday Presents.** Illus. by Suçie Stevenson. Orchard 1987. unpaged col illus.

  Loving parents describe their daughter's first six birthdays from the day she was born, when she screamed, through her fifth birthday celebration, when they had a dinosaur cake. Finally, before her sixth birthday, she gives them presents and funny cards on their birthdays and tells them that she loves them. (3–5)

- Rylant, Cynthia. **The Relatives Came.** Illus. by Stephen Gammell. Bradbury 1984. unpaged col illus.

  The relatives travel all day in an old station wagon from their rural mountain home to another dilapidated mountain home, where there is much hugging, loving, eating, music making and sleeping on the floor. Animated, colorful pencil drawings extend the uncomplicated story of family fun and love. (3–5)

- Segal, Lore. **Tell Me a Mitzi.** Pictures by Harriet Pincus. Farrar (h) Scholastic (p) 1970. unpaged col illus.

  "Tell me a story," Martha demands of her parents, and her mother and father tell three wonderful, hilarious stories about Mitzi and her precocious baby brother, Jacob. The stories are told with long run-on sentences that leave the reader breathless and add to the marvelous humor. (4–5)

  A series of three further adventures is told in **Tell Me a Trudy.**

- Viorst, Judith. **My Mama Says There Aren't Any Zombies, Ghosts, Vampires, Creatures, Demons, Monsters, Fiends, Goblins, or Things.** Illus. by Kay Chorao. Atheneum (h) Aladdin (p) 1973. 44p illus.

  Nick is sure there are monsters despite what Mama says, because in the past she's been wrong about a lot of things like when his tooth would fall out. Written in a very earnest, deadpan tone, this is hilariously funny. (3–5)

  In **Alexander and the Terrible, Horrible, No Good, Very Bad Day** *(illus. by Ray Cruz) a young boy is determined to run off to Australia after a day in which everything has gone wrong, but his mother convinces him that some days are bad even in Australia.*

  Blythe Danner's reading of five of Viorst's books and some of her verse is available from Harper Audio on the album entitled **Alexander and the Terrible, Horrible, No Good, Very Bad Day and Other Stories and Poems by Judith Viorst.**

- Williams, Vera B. **A Chair for My Mother.** Greenwillow (h&p) 1982. unpaged col illus.

  After their home has been destroyed by fire, a girl, her mother, and her grandmother keep their spare change in a large jar until they have enough to buy a large, flowery, and comfortable chair. Illustrated in bright, warm colors. (3–5)

In the sequel, **Something Special for Me,** the coin jar is emptied again to buy a very special birthday gift for Rosa, the young girl.

In **Music, Music for Everyone,** Rosa and her friends organize The Oak Street Band, play for parties, and use the money they earn for Grandma's medical treatment.

Siblings

- Banish, Roslyn. **Let Me Tell You about My Baby.** Harper (h&p) 1988. 56p b&w photos.

  A small boy expresses feelings of apprehension and jealousy about his mother's pregnancy and then about the new baby in his family, but he also feels love and pride when the baby smiles at him. (3–5)

- Blume, Judy. **Pain and the Great One.** Illus. by Irene Trivas. Bradbury (h) Dell (p) 1984. unpaged col illus.

  Two monologues, one by six-year-old Pain and the other by eight-year-old Great One, expound emphatically on the faults of and favors shown the other. Sibling rivalry at its funniest. (5)

- Brandenberg, Franz. **I Wish I Was Sick, Too.** Illus. by Aliki. Greenwillow 1976. unpaged col illus.

  Elizabeth envies Edward for all the attention he gets when he is sick and wishes she was sick as well. (4–5)

  Other books about Elizabeth and Edward are **A Secret for Grandmother's Birthday** *and* **A Robber, A Robber.**

- Bulla, Clyde Robert. **Keep Running, Allen!** Illus. by Satomi Ichikawa. Crowell 1978. unpaged col illus.

  Allen is the youngest of four children. He tries to keep up with his older siblings but is always lagging behind them. One day, in exhaustion, he lies down on the grass and discovers the quiet things there are to do, such as looking for shapes in the clouds. (4–5)

- Caines, Jeanette. **Abby.** Pictures by Steven Kellogg. Harper (h&p) 1973. 32p b&w illus.

  A realistic, loving story about Abby and her older brother, Kevin, who says he doesn't like girls but soon relents and admits he loves Abby, who was adopted and whom they can keep forever. (3–5)

- Cole, Joanna. **The New Baby at Your House.** Photos by Hella Hammid. Morrow (h&p) 1985. 48p b&w photos.

  An excellent discussion of what it means to have a new baby in the house, how the baby will behave and develop, and the feelings an older sibling may have. An extensive note to parents is also included. (2–5)

- De Lynam, Alicia Garcia. **It's Mine!** Dial 1988. unpaged col illus.

  The familiar sibling battle over a beloved toy is depicted in expressive, active watercolor illustrations with minimal text. (2–3)

- Fagerstrom, Grethe, and Gunilla Hansson. **Our New Baby: A Picture Story about Birth for Parents and Children.** Illus. by Gunilla Hansson. Barron's 1982. 48p col illus.

  Answers children's questions about babies from conception through birth and the impact of a new baby on the family. (4–5)

- Hazen, Barbara Shook. **Why Couldn't I Be an Only Kid Like You, Wigger?** Pictures by Leigh Grant. Atheneum (p) 1975. 31p illus.

  Wigger is visiting his friend, who belongs to a large family and envies Wigger for being an only child. His friend complains about the problems of being from such a large family and asks Wigger why he's always visiting them when it must be so great to be an only child. (5)

• Hughes, Shirley. **Dogger.** Morrow, 1988. unpaged col illus.

Dave is distressed when he loses his stuffed animal, Dogger. When he sees it on a sale table at a school fair, he can't afford to buy it back. His older sister lovingly helps him to get Dogger back. A heartwarming story of sibling cooperation and affection. (2–5)

• Hutchins, Pat. **Titch.** Macmillan (h&p) 1971. unpaged col illus.

Titch is the youngest of three children, and he always seems to get the short end of everything until one day his small share literally grows bigger and bigger. (2–5)

In the companion title, **You'll Soon Grow into Them, Titch,** *he finally gets some new clothes instead of the hand-me-downs he usually gets.*

• Hutchins, Pat. **The Very Worst Monster.** Greenwillow (h) Mulberry (p) 1985. unpaged col illus.

Everyone thinks the new baby is the worst monster in the world until his big sister, Hazel, tries to give him away. (3–5)

• Keats, Ezra Jack. **Peter's Chair.** Harper (h&p) 1967. unpaged col illus.

Peter and his dog, Willie, pack up and run away because his new baby sister is about to get his special chair. Peter is also featured in the author's other books, **The Snowy Day** *and* **Whistle for Willie.** (3–5)

• Kellogg, Steven. **Much Bigger than Martin.** Dial (h&p) 1976. 32p col illus.

A hilarious story about Henry, who fantasizes about being much bigger than his older brother in order to turn the tables on him. Younger siblings will delight in the exaggeration and the ending. (3–5)

- Kroll, Steven. **Friday the 13th.** Illus. by Dick Gackenbach. Holiday 1981. unpaged col illus.

  Hilda tauntingly tells her clumsy brother, Harold, that for him every day is like Friday the 13th. And she seems to be right—until a real Friday the 13th. (3–5)

- Lakin, Patricia. **Don't Touch My Room.** Illus. by Patience Brewster. Little, Brown 1985. 32p col illus.

  Aaron has a difficult time accepting the changes when his room is remodeled for his new brother, Benjamin. Eventually, he grows protective of his new sibling, and "Don't touch my room" becomes "Don't touch my baby." (3–5)

- Lexau, Joan N. **Emily and the Klunky Baby and the Next-Door Dog.** Pictures by Martha Alexander. Dial 1972. unpaged col illus.

  Emily's parents are divorced, and she and the klunky baby live with her mother. One morning her mother is too busy to help Emily make a snowman and tells her to look after the baby. Emily decides she'll run away to live with her father. (4–5)

- Marshall, Edward. **Fox and His Friends.** Dial (h&p) 1982. 56p col illus.

  Three stories about Fox involving his funny adventures with his younger sister, Louise. (4–5)

  This is available as a read-along kit from Listening Library. ▫▫

- Ormerod, Jan. **101 Things to Do with a Baby.** Lothrop (h) Puffin (p) 1984. unpaged col illus.

  Charming illustrations featuring a girl and her younger sibling accompany a list of one hundred and one simple, everyday ways to play with a baby. (0–5)

- Patent, Dorothy Hinshaw. **Babies!** Holiday 1988. 40p col photos.

  Appealing color photographs accompany a detailed text about the development of babies from birth through eighteen months. Interesting to older siblings. (4–5)

- Rogers, Fred. **The New Baby.** Photos by Jim Judkis. Putnam (h&p) 1985. unpaged col illus.

  A forthright and respectful discussion about how it feels to have a new sibling. (2–5)

- Steptoe, John. **Baby Says.** Lothrop 1988. unpaged col illus.

  An older boy's attempts to build a city with blocks are stymied by his infant brother's constant bids for attention. (0–2)

- Van Leeuwen, Jean. **Tales of Oliver Pig.** Illus. by Arnold Lobel. Dial (h&p) 1979. 64p col illus.

  The episodical adventures of this little boy pig are similar to common childhood experiences and focus on his relationships with his parents, his grandparents, and most particularly his younger sister, Amanda. The text is simple and straightforward, and the soft pencil drawings are appealing. (3–5)

  Other titles in the series include **More Tales of Oliver Pig, Amanda Pig and Her Big Brother Oliver, Tales of Amanda Pig,** *and* **More Tales of Amanda Pig.**

  Tales of Oliver Pig, More Tales of Oliver Pig, *and* **Amanda Pig and Her Big Brother Oliver** *are all available as read-along kits from Listening Library.* ◑◑

- Wells, Rosemary. **Max's First Word.** Dial 1979. unpaged col illus.

  Max persists in calling everything "bang" despite his sister Ruby's attempt to get him to do otherwise. (1–3)

  This small, brightly colored board book has several delightful companions: **Max's Toys: A Counting Book; Max's Ride; Max's New Suit; Max's Bath; Max's Birthday; Max's Breakfast; Max's Bedtime.**

- Wells, Rosemary. **Noisy Nora.** Dial (h&p) 1973. unpaged col illus.

  Nora gets lost in the middle between an older sister and a baby brother. She tries everything to get attention without success, so she leaves. But her absence finally gets her noticed. (4–5)

- Wells, Rosemary. **Peabody.** Dial (h&p) 1983. 32p col illus.

  Peabody enjoys being Annie's favorite toy and companion until she gets Rita, a walking and talking doll. But when Annie's brother, Robert, decides to give Rita a bath and ruins her, Annie turns to Peabody again. Peabody is a delightful, cuddly bear shown in the expressive color illustrations. (3–5)

Grandparents

- Flournoy, Valerie. **The Patchwork Quilt.** Illus. by Jerry Pinkney. Dial 1985. unpaged col illus.

  Each piece in the quilt Tanya's grandmother is making is the source of a family story. When the grandmother becomes ill, Tanya, and then the other members of the family, work to complete the patchwork of family memories. (5)

- Gomi, Taro. **Coco Can't Wait.** Morrow (h) Penguin (p) 1983. unpaged col illus.

  Traveling back and forth to see each other, Coco and her grandmother are always missing each other until one day they meet halfway. Simple humor and bright illustrations. (3–5)

- Hest, Amy. **Crack-of-Dawn Walkers.** Illus. by Amy Schwartz. Macmillan 1984. unpaged b&w illus.

  Sadie savors the Sundays when she and her grandfather get up early to go out for hot cocoa with whipped cream and he tells her stories of the old country. A quiet and loving story softly illustrated in black and white. (4–5)

- Hurd, Edith Thacher. **I Dance in My Red Pajamas.** Illus. by Emily Arnold McCully. Harper 1982. unpaged col illus.

  Jenny loves to spend the night at her grandparents', where she knows she'll dance merrily with her grandfather. Lively illustrations reinforce the carefree mood. (3–5)

• Levinson, Riki. **I Go with My Family to Grandma's.** Illus. by Diane Goode. Dutton 1986. unpaged col illus.

Five sets of cousins travel from the five boroughs of New York by bike, trolley, wagon, train, and ferry to Grandma's. An interesting glimpse of the city and transportation in turn-of-the-century New York City.

(4–5)

• Levinson, Riki. **Watch the Stars Come Out.** Illus. by Diane Goode. Dutton 1985. unpaged col illus.

Superb illustrations accompany the story of a young girl and her brother's emigration to the United States, related by the girl's great-granddaughter. *(4–5)*

• Oxenbury, Helen. **Grandma and Grandpa.** Dial 1984. unpaged col illus.

A little girl and her grandparents enjoy her weekend visits, but the grandparents are completely exhausted by the activity. *(2–5)*

• Rylant, Cynthia. **When I Was Young in the Mountains.** Illus. by Diane Goode. Dutton (h&p) 1982. 32p col illus.

Raised by her grandparents, a girl provides a lyrical recollection of her childhood in a rural area in the southern mountains, giving insight into a different type of lifestyle. *(4–5)*

A read-along kit is available from Miller-Brody/Random House. ▄▄

• Shulevitz, Uri. **Dawn.** Farrar 1974. 32p col illus.

A puddle of blue becomes a lake with a large tree under which a boy and his grandfather sleep. Dawn breaks as they rise, and as they take a boat out onto the lake, the sun rises in glorious colors. A work of art.

(3–5)

- Skorpen, Lisel Moak. **Mandy's Grandmother.** Pictures by Martha Alexander. Dial 1975. 32p col illus.

  Mandy and her grandmother overcome their generational differences and become great friends. (5)

- Stanovich, Betty Jo. **Big Boy, Little Boy.** Illus. by Virginia Wright-Frierson. Lothrop 1984. unpaged col illus.

  A warm, comfortable story about a young boy and his grandmother, who reminds him about the time when he couldn't write his name or stand on his head, but when she would tell him stories and sing him to sleep. Watercolor illustrations capture the loving relationship between child and grandparent. (2–5)

- Williams, Barbara. **Kevin's Grandma.** Illus. by Kay Chorao. Dutton 1975. unpaged col illus.

  Kevin has a grandmother who doesn't do the conventional grandmotherly things. Instead she rides a motorcycle, does judo and skydiving, and brings him Mad *magazine and homemade peanut-butter soup.* (4–5)

Growing Up

Young children grow fast. They grow faster physically over the first five years of life than they do at any other time, including adolescence. But in addition to gaining height, weight, and muscle control, they are also bent on establishing themselves as individuals. They want to do things for themselves. They want to eat what they want to eat when they want to eat it. Temper tantrums and the use of the word "NO" often are the twin symbols of their drive toward autonomy.

In their rush to explore and achieve, young children are fearless. They simply don't have the frame of reference to think through the consequences of a physical action. Adults gasp at their bravado, which is really egocentricity. This trait predominates through early childhood. It affects their relationships with their families and the people in the outside world with whom they are in contact.

Their maturational growth comes at a different rate. Neither size nor age are true indicators of maturity. Further, emotional growth is not as securely achieved as physical growth.

As children grow, the type and amount of attention needed from adults differ. Hindsight shows that infants are easy. Emotional support and encouragement to explore, to try something new, to learn to handle failure and success, require acknowledging and respecting children as individuals. No one ever said it was easy for either parents or children.

Becoming Independent

- Burningham, John. **The Blanket.** Crowell 1976. unpaged col illus.

  The search for a small boy's blanket so he can go to sleep is repeated in many homes. One in a series of small books on familiar themes that appeal to young children. *(1–4)*

  Other titles are: **The Baby, The Rabbit, The School, The Snow, The Dog, The Friend,** *and* **The Cupboard.**

- Cleary, Beverly. **The Growing-Up Feet.** Illus. by DyAnne Di-Salvo-Ryan. Morrow 1987. unpaged col illus.

  Twins Jimmy and Janet go to the shoe store but learn they aren't ready for new shoes yet. Their disappointment fades when their mother decides to buy them new red boots instead. *(3–5)*

- Cooney, Nancy Evans. **Donald Says Thumbs Down.** Illus. by Maxie Chambliss. Putnam 1987. unpaged col illus.

  When Donald decides to stop sucking his thumb, his parents support and encourage him. A very positively framed little story. *(3–5)*

- Hines, Anna Grossnickle. **All by Myself.** Clarion 1985. unpaged 2-col illus.

  Feeding herself and brushing her teeth are two big steps toward growing up, but a small girl also wants to stop wearing diapers at night. *(2–3)*

- Hoban, Russell. **Bread and Jam for Frances.** Illus. by Lillian Hoban. Harper (h&p) 1964. 31p col illus.

Frances's insatiable appetite for bread and jam, and only bread and jam, wanes when her mother follows her edict and gives her only bread and jam to eat. (2–5)
Frances the Badger appears in several other situations common to childhood, including **A Baby Sister For Frances, Bedtime for Frances,** *and* **A Birthday For Frances.** *All are available in both hardcover and paperback from Harper.*
Recordings of the Frances stories, **Frances** *and* **A Bargain for Frances and Other Frances Stories,** *read by Glynis Johns, are available from Harper Audio.* ◙

- Hoffman, Phyllis. **Baby's First Year.** Illus. by Sarah Wilson. Harper 1988. unpaged col illus.

Brief rhyming phrases and full-page pastel illustrations trace the major and minor events during baby's first year. (0–1)

- Hutchins, Pat. **Happy Birthday, Sam.** Greenwillow (h) Puffin (p) 1978. unpaged col illus.

Grandpa's birthday present gives Sam the independence he's longed for. Now he can turn on lights, open the front door, and even sail his boat in the sink. (2–5)

- Jonas, Ann. **Now We Can Go.** Greenwillow 1986. unpaged col illus.

"I'm not ready," a young child calls. Then item by item the box on the left-hand page is emptied into the bag on the right-hand page. With all her treasures packed, she finally calls "Now we can go!" (2–4)

- Jonas, Ann. **When You Were a Baby.** Greenwillow (h) Puffin (p) 1982. unpaged col illus.

Big, bright illustrations paired with spare text help young children realize just how much they can do now. (2–3)

- Klein, Norma. **Girls Can Be Anything.** Illus. by Roy Doty. Dutton (h&p) 1973. unpaged col illus.

  Marina disputes her kindergarten friend's decision that boys must have the leading roles in their games. (4–5)

- McPhail, David. **Pig Pig Grows Up.** Dutton (h&p) 1980. unpaged col illus.

  After being stubborn about giving up his crib, high chair, and stroller, Pig Pig grows up in a hurry. (3–5)

  A read-along kit is available from Live Oak Media.

- Oxenbury, Helen. **The Checkup.** Dial 1983. unpaged col illus.

  No longer sitting quietly in his mother's lap, a small boy wreaks havoc before and during his checkup. (2–5)

  Other titles in the series—**The Birthday Party, The Car Trip, The Dancing Class, Eating Out,** *and* **The First Day of School**—*reflect realistic contacts with the world away from home.*

- Rice, Eve. **New Blue Shoes.** Puffin (p) 1975. 32p col illus.

  Rebecca is not so sure her feet look right in the new shoes she said absolutely had to be blue. (3–5)

- Rockwell, Anne. **When We Grow Up.** Dutton 1981. unpaged col illus.

  First career choices of a group of young children reflect the various options, not limited by sex or race, available today. (3–5)

- Rogers, Fred. **Going to the Potty.** Photos by Jim Judkis. Putnam (h&p) 1986. unpaged col photos.

  Toilet training is presented in the matter-of-fact and supportive manner that one would expect from the host of the television show Mr. Rogers' Neighborhood. (2–3)

• Waber, Bernard. **Ira Sleeps Over.** Houghton Mifflin (h&p) 1972. 48p col illus.

Thrilled at the thought of spending the night at his friend Reggie's house, Ira becomes distressed at the thought of being without his beloved teddy bear. (5)

In **Ira Says Goodbye** *(1988) he learns that his best friend Reggie is moving away.*

This is available as a read-along kit from Live Oak Media. ▣

• Watanabe, Shigeo. **How Do I Put It On?** Illus. by Yasuo Ohtomo. Philomel (p) 1979. 28p col illus.

Getting dressed can be done two ways—right or wrong. A small bear shows them both. (2–5)

Other titles in the series (most available in both hardcover and paper from Philomel) are **Daddy, Play with Me!; Get Set! Go!; I Can Build a House; I Can Ride It; I Can Take a Bath; I Can Take a Walk; I'm the King of the Castle; What a Good Lunch;** *and* **Where's My Daddy?**

• Winthrop, Elizabeth. **Bear and Mrs. Duck.** Illus. by Patience Brewster. Holiday 1988. unpaged col illus.

Bear is very upset when Nora leaves him with Mrs. Duck, but eventually he warms up to his feathered baby-sitter. Charming illustrations of Mrs. Duck in a wide-brimmed hat flying up to get a book from a high shelf and swimming in the bathtub add humor. (3–5)

- Zolotow, Charlotte. **I Like to Be Little.** Illus. by Erik Blegvad. Crowell 1987. unpaged col illus.

  A dialogue between a small girl and her mother lists the reasons a little girl thinks it is fun to be little. Charming new illustrations capture the carefree nature of childhood in this story, which was originally published with the title **I Want To Be Little.** (3–5)

- Zolotow, Charlotte. **William's Doll.** Illus. by William Pène Du Bois. Harper (h&p) 1972. 30p col illus.

  William loves to play basketball and has great fun with his electric trains, but he also wants a doll even though his father and brother say "Dolls are sissy." (2–5)

Responsible and Safe Behavior

- Ancona, George. **Helping Out.** Clarion 1985. unpaged b&w photos.

  Well-designed black-and-white photographs show how children can and do help within their families and within their communities.   (3–5)

- Bottner, Barbara. **Messy.** Delacorte 1979. unpaged col illus.

  Thrilled because she's been chosen to be the princess in her ballet class's recital, Harriet is determined to be neat rather than her usual messy self.   (5)

- Brown, Marc Tolon and Stephen Krensky. **Dinosaurs, Beware: A Safety Guide.** Atlantic/Little, Brown (h&p) 1982. unpaged col illus.

  Cartoonlike illustrations starring dinosaurs show what happens when safety rules are not followed.   (3–5)

- Cole, Brock. **No More Baths.** Doubleday 1980. unpaged col illus.

  Baths are bad enough at night, but when her parents want her to take one during the day, Jessie McWhistle runs away until she realizes home has her favorite food and her bed.   (2–5)

- Goodsell, Jane. **Toby's Toe.** Illus. by Gioia Fiammenghi. Morrow 1986. unpaged col illus.

  Toby wakes up, stubs his toe, and pops his sister's blue balloon, which sets off a chain of events with far-reaching and unhappy results. Later in the day he starts another, happier chain.   (4–5)

- Hoban, Russell. **Dinner at Alberta's.** Pictures by James Marshall. Crowell (h) Dell (p) 1975. 40p b&w illus.

  A crush on his sister's friend Alberta encourages young Arthur Croco-dile to change his rowdy ways. (5)

  A read-along kit is available from Listening Library. ●●

- Joslin, Sesyle. **What Do You Say, Dear?** Illus. by Maurice Sendak. Harper (h&p) 1958. unpaged col illus.

  Snippets of text and humorous illustrations enliven this tongue-in-cheek guide to manners. While children would never be in similar situations, they do grasp the concept of appropriate behavior. (4–5)

  The companion title, **What Do You Do, Dear?** *(h&p), is equally funny.*

- Lionni, Leo. **The Biggest House in the World.** Pantheon (h&p) 1968. unpaged col illus.

  A small snail's longing for a huge house becomes modified after he hears about the snail who has a glorious, large house but who cannot move. Spare text and lovely illustrations make this moral tale very palatable. (4–5)

  A read-along kit is available from Random House. ●●

- McLeod, Emilie Warren. **Bear's Bicycle.** Illus. by David McPhail. Little, Brown (h) Puffin (p) 1975. 31p col illus.

  While his teddy bear (who's suddenly grown to gargantuan proportions) careens wildly, a little boy shows how to ride a bike safely. (3–5)

- Peet, Bill. **Big Bad Bruce.** Houghton Mifflin (h&p) 1977. 38p col illus.

  Thinking he can intimidate everyone on the mountain, Big Bruce finds he's made a mistake when one of the boulders he sends rolling down the hill comes within a hair's breadth of hitting Roxy, a witch, who's perfectly prepared to teach him some manners. (2–5)

- Sharmat, Marjorie Weinman. **I'm Terrific.** Illus. by Kay Chorao. Holiday (h) Scholastic (p) 1977. 28p col illus.

Jason Everett Bear knows he's the best. The other animals think he's a know-it-all and want nothing to do with him until he changes his attitude. (3–5)

- Simon, Norma. **What Do I Say?.** Illus. by Joe Lasker. Whitman 1967. unpaged col illus.

Pictures of common occurrences in Manuel's home life and school day set the scene for the simple text to answer the question posed by the title. (3–5)

- Waber, Bernard. **An Anteater Named Arthur.** Houghton Mifflin (h&p) 1967. 46p col illus.

Fussy, messy, and absentminded, Arthur is a problematic anteater child. (4–5)

Friendship

- Alexander, Sue. **Witch, Goblin, and Sometimes Ghost: Six Read-Alone Stories.** Pictures by Jeanette Winter. Pantheon 1976. 59p b&w illus.

  Sometimes fearful, sometimes absentminded, sometimes out of sorts, Goblin is lucky enough to have two good friends, Witch and Ghost, who inevitably will come to his aid. (3–5)

  Additional titles in this series are **More Witch, Goblin, and Ghost Stories** *and* **Witch, Goblin and Ghost in the Haunted Woods.**

- Aliki. **We Are Best Friends.** Greenwillow 1982. 32p col illus.

  After his best friend Peter moves away, Robert just mopes around. The new boy in his class is an unlikely candidate for friendship until Robert comes to see that he and Will have interests in common. (4–5)

- Carle, Eric. **Do You Want to Be My Friend?** Crowell 1971. unpaged col illus.

  A small mouse eager for friendship addresses his question to a series of tails, each attached to a large animal too busy to be bothered with him, until he finally finds another mouse who cheerfully agrees. The bright pictures and the simplicity of the text endear this little book to its large audience. (1–5)

- Delton, Judy. **Two Good Friends.** Illus. by Giulio Maestro. Crown (p) 1974. 32p col illus.

  The two friends, Duck and Bear, have quite different skills. Duck keeps a very tidy house but can't cook. Bear provides good food but is a sloppy housekeeper. Rather than continuously feeling frustrated by each other's inadequacies, they decide to supplement each other's strengths. (3–5)

• Feder, Jane. **My Cat Beany.** Illus. by Karen Gundersheimer. Knopf (h&p) 1979. unpaged col illus.

In endearing text and illustrations Jonathan tells about his cat and best friend, Beany. (2–5)

• Fox, Mem. **Wilfrid Gordon MacDonald Partridge.** Illus. by Julie Vivas. Kane-Miller 1985. unpaged col illus.

The young boy with the four-part name is fond of the older adults who live next door, but he is fondest of the elderly woman who also has four parts to her name. Miss Nancy frets about her loss of memory, and the boy tries to help her by first finding out what a memory is—different people have different answers—and then getting some for her. An absolute gem of a book. (4–5)

• Graham, Bob. **Pete and Roland.** Viking (p) 1984. unpaged col illus.

Understated cartoonlike drawings tell a large part of the story of the friendship between Pete and a lost parakeet, Roland. (4–5)

• Henkes, Kevin. **Chester's Way.** Greenwillow 1988. unpaged col illus.

Chester and Wilson are best friends who share a methodical and precise approach to life. Then they meet Lilly, who "has a mind of her own," but she becomes their friend nevertheless. An amusing story about friendship and individual differences. (3–5)

- Henkes, Kevin. **A Weekend with Wendell.** Greenwillow 1986. unpaged col illus.

  When Wendell spends the weekend at Sophie's house while his parents are out of town, he makes the rules for all the games and causes so much mischief that each night she's glad he's closer to going home. She finally sets up a game that establishes their friendship. (4–5)

- Hoff, Syd. **Who Will Be My Friends?** Harper (h&p) 1960. 32p col illus.

  Moving to a new home means finding new friends. While Freddy is worried at first, he discovers that his fears have been for naught. (3–5)

- Lionni, Leo. **Alexander and the Wind-Up Mouse.** Pantheon 1969. unpaged col illus.

  A real mouse finds his arrival comes in a very poor second to that of his friend—a wind-up mouse. (3–5)

- Lobel, Arnold. **Frog and Toad Are Friends.** Harper (h&p) 1972. 64p col illus.

  Critics and children alike enjoy the humorous and easy-to-read short stories about the bumptious friends. (2–5)

  Other titles about this duo are **Frog and Toad Together, Frog and Toad All Year,** *and* **Days with Frog and Toad.**

  The read-along kits from Harper for each title feature the author's expressive voice. ◼◼

- Rogers, Fred. **Making Friends.** Photos by Jim Judkis. Putnam (h&p) 1987. unpaged col photos.

  A frank discussion, as one would expect from television's Mr. Rogers, about the rewards and the difficulties of friendship, including learning to share and feeling angry or sad. (3–5)

- Sharmat, Marjorie Weinman. **I'm Not Oscar's Friend Anymore.** Illus. by Tony DeLuna. Dutton 1975. 32p col illus.

  The narrator imagines that his former friend Oscar is pining away without him after their big fight. When he calls Oscar to give him the chance to make up, Oscar has forgotten their fight and they make plans to play again. (3–5)

- Steptoe, John. **Stevie.** Harper (h&p) 1969. unpaged col illus.

  When Robert's mother starts caring for Stevie during the week, Robert is mightily annoyed. His constant complaints about the younger child's behavior fade away after Stevie's family moves, and Robert, to his surprise, realizes he misses the boy. The tender tone of the story and the Roualt-like illustrations of Steptoe's first book, published when he was only 18, established him as a strong talent in the children's book world. (4–5)

- Stevenson, James. **Fast Friends.** Greenwillow (h) Scholastic (p) 1979. 64p col illus.

  Murray the turtle and Fred the snail are both poky. They never get to play in games with the other animals until they find a skateboard and startle the others with their prowess. (3–5)

- Vincent, Gabrielle. **Breakfast Time, Ernest and Celestine.** Greenwillow 1982, 1985. unpaged col illus.

  Young Celestine Mouse makes a real mess at the breakfast table one morning, but Ernest Bear calmly helps her clean up. The gentle story is told entirely through soft watercolor illustrations. (1–5)

  In **Ernest and Celestine's Patchwork Quilt** *Celestine decides she wants a quilt for her bed after she sees how nicely the quilt for Ernest's bed has turned out.*

• Vincent, Gabrielle. **Ernest and Celestine's Picnic.** Greenwillow 1982. unpaged col illus.

Disappointed when their planned picnic appears to be rained out, Celestine is overjoyed when Ernest says they'll go anyway. They'll just wear raincoats and boots and use a tarpaulin instead of a blanket.

(0–5)

Other titles in this very popular Ernest and Celestine series are **Bravo, Ernest and Celestine; Smile, Ernest and Celestine;** *and* **Where Are You, Ernest and Celestine?**

• Wittman, Sally. **A Special Trade.** Illus. by Karen Gundersheimer. Harper (h&p) 1978. unpaged col illus.

A very special friendship has existed between Old Bartholomew and young Nelly ever since she was a baby. Their very real respect for each other has made this one of the all-time popular titles with both children and adults. *(2–5)*

• Zolotow, Charlotte. **I Know a Lady.** Illus. by James Stevenson. Greenwillow (h) Puffin (p) 1984. unpaged col illus.

A friend can be any age, and when you have a neighbor who is interested enough to give you treats and share special occasions, it doesn't matter that she's much older than you are. *(3–5)*

Individual Differences

- Brandenberg, Franz. **Otto Is Different.** Illus. by James Stevenson. Greenwillow 1985. unpaged col illus.

  Unhappy because his eight arms make him different from his friends, Otto discovers there are times when being different is a very good thing to be. (3–5)

- Brown, Tricia. **Someone Special, Just Like You.** Photos by Fran Ortiz. Henry Holt 1984. 64p b&w photos.

  Physically and mentally handicapped youngsters are shown actively and joyfully participating in a variety of activities. The expressive photographs are effectively paired with a simple text. (3–5)

- Caple, Kathy. **The Biggest Nose.** Houghton Mifflin 1985. 32p col illus.

  Constantly made fun of because of her nose, Eleanor, a young elephant, at first attempts to change her appearance, until she realizes that each tormentor has a large feature also. (3–5)

- Clifton, Lucille. **My Friend Jacob.** Illus. by Thomas di Grazia. Dutton 1980. unpaged illus.

  The unlikely friendship between seven-year-old Sam and mentally handicapped sixteen-year-old Jacob is beneficial to each of them. This gentle story of true friendship is enhanced by the soft-toned pencil illustrations. (5)

- Cooney, Barbara. **Miss Rumphius.** Viking (h) Puffin (p) 1982. unpaged col illus.

  Great-Aunt Alice has had an unusual life, and now she continues the pattern by making the world a more beautiful place. The stunning paintings draw the attention of the young child and adult alike. (4–5)

- Greene, Laura. **I Am Somebody.** Photos by Gerald Cross. Childrens Press (h&p) 1980. 30p col photos.

  Nathan loves to play baseball, but he's never chosen first and inevitably drops an important catch or is thrown out at the base. He finally comes to realize he doesn't have to be good in all activities that he enjoys. (5)

- Kraus, Robert. **Leo the Late Bloomer.** Illus. by Jose Aruego. Crowell (h&p) 1971. 32p col illus.

  Leo sees all the things his friends can do and is unhappy, but he really gets distressed when his father comments on his slowness. Many children are concerned when they don't keep up with their peers and will be reassured by Leo's mother's calm and accurate advice to be patient. (2–5)

- Levine, Edna S. **Lisa and her Soundless World.** Illus. by Gloria Kamen. Human Sciences (h&p) 1974. 34p col illus.

  Even though Lisa is deaf, she and her family can live a regular life by making a few adjustments. (5)

- Rabe, Berniece. **Balancing Girl.** Illus. by Lillian Hoban. Dutton 1981. unpaged col illus.

  Margaret may use crutches and a wheelchair, but she's full of good ideas and doesn't let her physical handicap stop her from participating in the activities of her first-grade class. (5)

- Reich, Hanns. **Children of Many Lands.** Hill & Wang (p) 1958. 120p b&w photos.

  The attractive photographic essay shows that children all over the world enjoy doing much the same things. (4–5)

- Say, Allen. **Bicycle Man.** Houghton Mifflin 1982. unpaged col illus.

  The students, teachers, and parents of a small rural school in Japan are enjoying the first sports day after the end of World War II when the arrival of two American soldiers causes consternation. The mood changes quickly as one of the soldiers puts on a bicycle-stunt exhibition while his friend shouts encouragement. (4–5)

- Wells, Rosemary. **Shy Charles.** Dial 1988. unpaged col illus.

  Charles is an excruciatingly shy mouse, and his parents' attempts to draw him out with ballet lessons and football practice are embarrassing failures. But when Mrs. Block, the baby-sitter, falls down the stairs, Charles doesn't hesitate to help her—although he shuns the subsequent praise and gratitude. (4–5)

Coping

- Aliki. **Two of Them.** Greenwillow 1979. unpaged col illus.

  A little girl and her grandfather have a special, close relationship. As she grows older and he ages, she lovingly cares for him. After his death the girl mourns him and thinks about his memory. (4–5)

- Bonsall, Crosby. **Who's Afraid of the Dark?** Harper (h&p) 1980. 32p col illus.

  Afraid of the dark, a small boy tries to convince his dog not to be frightened. (2–5)

- Brown, Laurene Krasny, and Marc Tolon Brown. **Dinosaurs Divorce: A Guide for Changing Families.** Illus. by Marc Tolon Brown. Joy Street/Little, Brown 1986. 31p col illus.

  The concerns felt by young children of divorcing or divorced parents are dealt with in a reassuring and matter-of-fact manner that happens to feature dinosaurs in the illustrations. (3–5)

- Brown, Margaret Wise. **Dead Bird.** Illus. by Remy Charlip. Harper 1958. unpaged col illus.

  Several children find a dead bird, describe how they determine it is truly dead, and have a touching burial and funeral for it. A dignified and matter-of-fact portrayal of children dealing with death. (4–5)

- Caseley, Judith. **When Grandpa Came to Stay.** Greenwillow 1986. unpaged col illus.

  Benny loves having his Grandpa visit, but is upset one night when his grandfather begins to cry because he misses his wife, who has died. Very openly deals with a child's reaction to an adult's grief. (4–5)

- Clifton, Lucille. **Everett Anderson's Goodbye.** Illus. by Ann Grifalconi. Henry Holt (h&p) 1983. unpaged b&w illus.

  Everett Anderson goes through the stages of grieving—denial, anger, bargaining, depression, and finally acceptance—after the death of his father. (5)

- Cohen, Miriam. **Jim's Dog Muffin.** Illus. by Lillian Hoban. Greenwillow (h) Dell (p) 1984. unpaged col illus.

  Jim's classmates try to console him when his dog is run over by a truck; finally his friend Paul breaks through his grief. An uncondescending treatment about dealing with loss and allowing time for mourning. (4–5)

- Crowe, Robert L. **Clyde Monster.** Illus. by Kay Chorao. Dutton 1976. 32p col illus.

  Clyde is a monster child who refuses to go to bed one night because he is afraid there are people in his dark cave waiting to get him. (4–5)

- Jonas, Ann. **Holes and Peeks.** Greenwillow 1984. unpaged col illus.

  From a child's point of view, holes are scary and peeks are fun. But holes can be mended or plugged, as the young child who narrates this simple text explains. (2–5)

- Klein, Norma. **Visiting Pamela.** Illus. by Kay Chorao. Dial 1979. unpaged b&w illus.

  Carrie dreads staying at Pamela's house after school for the first time, and indeed the afternoon does not start off well. Things improve, and Carrie decides that she might like to visit again after all. *(4–5)*

- Perry, Patricia, and Marietta Lynch. **Mommy and Daddy Are Divorced.** Dial (h&p) 1978. unpaged b&w photos.

Ned and his brother Joey live with their mother, as their parents are divorced. They are happy to see their father when he visits and upset when he leaves. Both parents deal openly and lovingly with the boys' feelings. *(5)*

- Raskin, Ellen. **Nothing Ever Happens on My Block.** Atheneum (p) 1966. unpaged col illus.

Chester, a singularly unobservant boy, complains that nothing ever happens in his neighborhood. If he would just turn around, he would see children playing, a house burning, robbers, and a parachutist landing. *(3–5)*

- Raskin, Ellen. **Spectacles.** Atheneum (p) 1968. unpaged col illus.

No one understands why Iris keeps seeing strange things like fire-breathing dragons and giant pygmy nuthatches until her mother takes her to a doctor whom Iris sees as a blue elephant until he prescribes glasses for her. *(4–5)*

- Rogers, Fred. **Moving.** Photos by Jim Judkis. Putnam 1987. unpaged col photos.

Explores the concerns of young children regarding a household move, from packing and leaving familiar surroundings to settling into a new house and neighborhood. The subject is presented in the reassuring and honest tone that has become the hallmark of the "Mr. Rogers" television series. *(2–5)*

- Sharmat, Marjorie Weinman. **Gila Monsters Meet You at the Airport.** Illus. by Byron Barton. Macmillan (h) Puffin (p) 1980. unpaged col illus.

  Apprehensive about moving west from Manhattan, a young boy is sure there will be cactus everywhere, that kids will ride horses to school, and that everyone will be too busy chasing buffaloes to play baseball. When the plane lands, he meets a boy with similar concerns about moving east—only he worries about gangsters, snow, planes zooming through his apartment, and alligators escaping from the sewers. (4–5)

- Simon, Norma. **I Was So Mad.** Illus. by Dora Leder. Whitman 1974. 40p col illus.

  Many different situations that make children angry are shown in a non-judgmental manner that helps children to understand their anger and frustration and discover appropriate ways of dealing with them. (3–5)

- Tobias, Tobi. **Moving Day.** Pictures by William Pène du Bois. Knopf 1976. 29p col illus.

  A young girl describes the preparation, packing, and good-byes involved in leaving a familiar home and the long trip and arrival at her new home. A beloved stuffed bear provides the reassurance needed for the transition. (4–5)

- Townsend, Maryann, and Ronnie Stern. **Pop's Secret.** Lippincott 1980. 26p b&w photos.

  Photos from a family album show the progression from infancy to old age, including the relationship between a young boy and his grandfather. When the grandfather dies, the family remembers him lovingly. (5)

- Tyler, Linda Wagner. **The Sick-in-Bed Birthday.** Illus. by Susan Davis. Viking/Kestrel 1988. unpaged col illus.

  Plans to celebrate a birthday are abruptly changed when Tucky comes down with the chicken pox on the all-important day. (2–5)

- Viorst, Judith. **The Tenth Good Thing about Barney.** Illus. by Erik Blegvad. Atheneum (h&p) 1971. 25p b&w illus.

  To help him deal with the death of his pet cat, Barney, a mother suggests that a small boy think of ten good things about Barney to say at a funeral for him. (5)

- Zolotow, Charlotte. **My Grandson Lew.** Pictures by William Pène du Bois. Harper (h&p) 1974. 30p col illus.

  Six-year-old Lewis awakens in the night and surprises his mother by talking about his grandfather, who died when Lewis was two. This was one of the first books published on the theme of the death of a grandparent, and it remains one of the most memorable and hauntingly beautiful titles available. (4–5)

School

- Beim, Jerrold. **The Smallest Boy in the Class.** Illus. by Meg Wohlberg. Morrow 1949. unpaged col illus.

  Feeling he's got to make his presence felt because he's the smallest boy in the class, Tiny makes more noise, draws the biggest pictures, and tells the most outlandish tales. He does come to feel he has something positive to contribute without being obnoxious. (4–5)

- Brandenberg, Franz. **No School Today.** Illus. by Aliki. Macmillan (p) 1975. 32p col illus.

  When Edward and Elizabeth get to school very early one morning, no one is there. They incorrectly assume there is no school and run home to tell everyone, including their teachers and the principal. (5)

- Breinburg, Petronella. **Shawn Goes to School.** Illus. by Errol Lloyd. Crowell 1973. unpaged col illus.

  Shawn finally gets to go to nursery school, but when his mother and sister try to leave him there, he screams. As he realizes that the teacher and other children are friendly, he calms down and even smiles a little. (3–5)

- Cohen, Miriam. **Will I Have a Friend?** Illus. by Lillian Hoban. Macmillan (h&p) 1967. unpaged col illus.

  Jim is worried about the first day of school and particularly whether he will find a friend there. (5)

  Other titles by the author about the same characters include **No Good in Art**—*Greenwillow (h), Dell (p)—and* **When Will I Read?**—*Greenwillow (h) Dell (p).*

- Isadora, Rachel. **Willaby.** Macmillan 1977. 32p col illus.

  Willaby draws all the time and everywhere. Instead of copying a get-well poem for her teacher, she draws a picture but forgets to sign her name. She worries that her teacher won't know it's from her and will think Willaby doesn't like her. A happy resolution awaits her at school the following day. (4–5)

- McCully, Emily Arnold. **School.** Harper 1987. unpaged col illus.

  On an autumn morning a young mouse watches all her siblings go to school, leaving her alone at home with her mother. She decides to follow them to school and joins the class until her mother retrieves her. Told entirely in colorful pictures. (3–5)

- Radlauer, Ruth Shaw. **Molly.** Illus. by Emily Arnold McCully. Prentice-Hall 1987. unpaged col illus.

  A rumpled Molly gets ready for school in the morning and rides the bus to nursery school, where she plays with blocks, paints, and rides a tricycle. She arrives home with blue paint on her face and blouse, untied shoelaces, and a big smile. Expressive illustrations, an understated text, and small size make this an appealing title. (3–5)

- Rockwell, Harlow. **My Nursery School.** Greenwillow 1976. unpaged col illus.

  This is a simple, uncluttered introduction to nursery school. (2–4)

- Rogers, Fred. **Going to Day Care.** Photos by Jim Judkis. Putnam (h&p) 1985. unpaged col photos.

  Designed to help children anticipate what will happen in a day-care situation, the text and photographs provide insight, warmth, and gentleness. (1–5)

- Schwartz, Amy. **Annabelle Swift, Kindergartner.** Orchard 1988. unpaged col illus.

  On instructions from her sister, Lucy, Annabelle answers the roll call "Annabelle Swift, Kindergartner," calls red "raving scarlet" and blue "blue desire," and is embarrassed when her answers don't quite seem right. But when it comes time to count the milk money, Annabelle is the only one who knows how and is proud to be chosen to take the money to the cafeteria. (5)

- Tyler, Linda Wagner. **Waiting for Mom.** Illus. by Susan Davis. Viking 1987. unpaged col illus.

  A young hippo anxiously waits for his mother to pick him up after school. He spends time in the library and the principal's office and finally on the front steps watching a clock and every car that goes by. Finally his mother arrives and explains why she was unavoidably late. (4–5)

- Wiseman, Bernard. **Morris Goes to School.** Harper (h&p) 1970. 64p col illus.

  Morris the moose tries to buy candy at the fish store and can't count the money when he tries to buy gumdrops. To remedy the situation, he decides to go to school, where he can learn to read and count. (4–5)

Information, Please!

Young children ask questions before they can talk. After they start talking, What? How? Why? pepper their conversation. Their questions about the world they want so desperately to know should be answered honestly. Today there are the resources to do it.

Fiction is not the only form of literature, despite what some might say. A different sense of satisfaction is gained from reading an information book. It is similar in mood to working on a jigsaw puzzle. As the pieces fit in, an incomplete picture becomes whole.

In the adult book world nonfiction sells better than fiction. For some strange reason young children are not exposed to information books as regularly and as consistently as they are told stories. They are, in effect, cut off from learning that learning is fun. Today's nonfiction books are visually attractive as well as informative. Many are written in a lively tone that captures the author's own excitement about the subject.

There are many children who are more interested in information than story. Follow their preferences. Read them books about cars, trains, animals, stars, or digging through the earth. Reading then becomes a joyful activity they want to pursue.

Home and Community

- Anno, Mitsumasa. **Anno's U.S.A.** Philomel 1983. unpaged col illus.

  This visual journey across the United States compresses historical and cultural events and people into vignettes set into the detailed double-page spread illustrations. Young children pick out the scenes easily, but adults must do the identification. (3–5)

  Other titles available in hardcover and paper on the same country/culture theme are **Anno's Journey, Anno's Italy,** *and* **Anno's Britain.**

- Barton, Byron. **Building a House.** Greenwillow (h) Puffin (p) 1981. unpaged col illus.

  Outlines how a house is built in brightly colored illustrations and simple, informative text. (1–5)

- Barton, Byron. **Machines at Work.** Crowell 1987. unpaged col illus.

  A crew of men and women operates a crane, bulldozer, jackhammers, dumptruck, and other heavy equipment. The brightly hued illustrations boldly outlined in black have immense appeal. (1–5)

- Berger, Melvin. **Switch On, Switch Off.** Illus. by Carolyn Croll. Crowell 1989. 32p col illus.

  How electricity is generated is given a clear explanation and further illustrated with a simple experiment using a magnet and a coil of wire. (4–5)

- Bester, Roger. **Fireman Jim.** Crown 1981. unpaged b&w photos.

  A fireman's day and night spent at the fire station and fighting a fire are depicted in photos and simple text.   (3–5)

- Crews, Donald. **Light.** Greenwillow 1981. unpaged col illus.

  Striking, bright illustrations and brief identifying text show the different natural and man-made sources of light after dark.   (2–5)

- Gibbons, Gail. **Department Store.** Crowell (h) Harper (p) 1984. unpaged col illus.

  The activities behind the scenes and on the sales floor of a large department store are shown in detailed, colorful pictures.   (3–5)

- Gibbons, Gail. **Fire! Fire!** Crowell (h) Harper (p) 1984. unpaged col illus.

  Describes fire-fighting methods in the city, country, and forest as well as on the waterfront, with detailed, action-filled illustrations.   (3–5)

- Gibbons, Gail. **The Post Office Book: Mail and How It Moves.** Crowell (h) Harper (p) 1982. unpaged col illus.

  How the mail moves from sender to receiver is detailed in brief text and bright red-white-and-blue illustrations.   (4–5)

- Gibbons, Gail. **Tool Book.** Holiday 1982. unpaged col illus.

  Flat, colorful illustrations of various labeled tools grouped by the work they do and shown in action, together with a brief text, provide a comprehensive introduction to familiar tools.   (2–5)

- Gibbons, Gail. **Tunnels.** Holiday 1984. unpaged col illus.

  The author-artist provides colorful diagrams of a variety of tunnels made by animals and humans, with simple explanations about their construction.   (4–5)

- Hoban, Tana. **Dig, Drill, Dump, Fill.** Greenwillow 1975. 32p b&w photos.

  Cranes, dump trucks, and garbage trucks are among the heavy-duty machines pictured at work here in full-page black-and-white photos. The only text is a pictorial dictionary at the end of the book, which names each machine and briefly describes what it does. (2–5)

- Jonas, Ann. **Round Trip.** Greenwillow (h) Scholastic (p) 1983. unpaged b&w illus.

  Creative black-and-white illustrations depict a journey from the country into the city. Turn the book upside down and go from back to front for the return trip. (3–5)

- Martin, Charles E. **Island Winter.** Greenwillow 1984. unpaged col illus.

  Shows what the children who live year round on a coastal island do during the winter. Pleasant watercolor illustrations depict their homes, the one-room school, and the gentle pace of life. (4–5)

  *In **Summer Business** the island is crowded with tourists, and the children devise various businesses to raise money to visit the mainland.*

- Robbins, Ken. **City/Country: A Car Trip in Photographs.** Viking/Kestrel 1985. unpaged col photos.

  A car trip from the city and through the countryside is shown in soft, hand-tinted photographs. (3–5)

- Rockwell, Anne. **I Like the Library.** Dutton 1977. unpaged col illus.

  Introduces the various services and materials available at a library and borrowing procedures as a young boy tells about his visit. (1–5)

- Rockwell, Anne. **Our Garage Sale.** Illus. by Harlow Rockwell. Greenwillow 1984. unpaged col illus.

  A young boy tells about the many things in his family's attic, cellar, and garage that are no longer needed or used and describes the garage sale they decide to have in order to sell them. (3–5)

- Rockwell, Anne and Harlow. **Nice and Clean.** Macmillan 1984. unpaged col illus.

  The many everyday materials and tools used in housecleaning are shown in uncluttered watercolor illustrations and brief text as a young child, mother, and father demonstrate their use. (3–5)

- Rockwell, Anne and Harlow. **Supermarket.** Macmillan 1979. unpaged col illus.

  Shows how items are arranged in a grocery store as a mother and small child do their shopping. (1–5)

- Schaaf, Peter. **Apartment House Close Up.** Macmillan/Four Winds 1980. unpaged b&w photos.

  Few words and numerous photographs of the interior and exterior of an apartment house depict this specific type of housing. (3–5)

Health and the Human Body

- Balestrino, Philip. **The Skeleton Inside You**, rev. ed. Illus. by True Kelley. Crowell (h) Harper (p) 1989. 32p col illus.

  A lucid introduction to the human skeleton, including discussions of how it gives us shape and helps us move, what bones are made of, what happens when a bone breaks, and what foods help bones grow. *(4–5)*

- Berger, Melvin. **Germs Make Me Sick.** Illus. by Marylin Hafner. Crowell (h) Harper (p) 1985. 32p col illus.

  Achy arms and legs, a headache, a fever, and a sore throat are caused by tiny, tiny germs. Just where the viruses and bacteria live and how they cause illness are explained in an easily understood manner. (4–5)

- Brenner, Barbara. **Bodies.** Photos and design by George Ancona. Dutton 1973. unpaged b&w photos.

  An exploration in photographs of different body types and how the body works. *(3–5)*

  Faces, *in a similar format, focuses on the sensory organs.*

- Cole, Joanna. **How You Were Born.** Morrow (h&p) 1984. 48p b&w photos.

  Black-and-white photographs and diagrams accompany a concise, factual text explaining the development of the fetus before birth. Also described is birth itself, including Caesarean section. *(4–5)*

- DeSantis, Kenny. **A Doctor's Tools.** Photos by Patricia A. Agre. Dodd, Mead (h&p) 1985. 47p b&w photos.

  A doctor's tools are a source of curiosity and concern to young children. Photos and brief text help to answer questions and allay some of the concern. (2–5)

- Kuklin, Susan. **When I See My Dentist . . .** Bradbury Press 1988. unpaged col photos.

  This title and its companion, **When I See My Doctor,** *are excellent presentations of routine dental and medical visits as told from a young child's point of view. Each deals with the special instruments and equipment, combining close-up photographs with discussions about what they're used for and what they feel like.* (3–5)

- Marino, Barbara Pavis. **Eric Needs Stitches.** Photos by Richard Rudinski. Lippincott 1979. 28p b&w photos.

  Eric goes to the emergency room for a bad cut received in a fall from his bike. The emergency-room procedures, including those involved in stitching up his knee, are carefully explained. (4–5)

- Parramon, J. M., and J. J. Puig. **Taste.** Illus. by Maria Rius. Barron's (p) 1985. unpaged col illus.

  Large, attractive illustrations accompany a very simple introduction to the sense of taste that concludes with a more detailed page of text and a diagram of the tongue. (3–5)

  Similar treatment is given to the other senses in **Hearing, Smell, Touch,** *and* **Sight.**

- Rey, Margret and H. A. **Curious George Goes to the Hospital.** In collaboration with the Children's Hospital Medical Center, Boston. Houghton Mifflin 1966. 48p col illus.

  George swallows a piece of a jigsaw puzzle and goes to the hospital, where he undergoes several procedures including an X ray and an operation. Useful preparation for a child's hospital visit. (2–5)

- Rockwell, Harlow. **My Dentist.** Greenwillow (h) Mulberry (p) 1975. unpaged col illus.

A young girl describes her first visit to the dentist. Minimal text and attractive illustrations depict the tools and procedures. A reassuring tone helps to prepare young children for a first visit to the dentist.

(3–5)

A companion to **My Doctor.**

- Rogers, Fred. **Going to the Hospital.** Photos by Jim Judkis. Putnam 1988. unpaged col photos.

This honest and reassuring preparation for a child's visit to the hospital emphasizes the validity of the child's feelings and the importance of discussing those feelings. Includes a note for parents. *(3–5)*

- Sheffield, Margaret. **Where Do Babies Come From?** Illus. by Sheila Bewley. Knopf 1973. 33p col illus.

Gentle text and soft, filmy illustrations convey the basic facts about human sexuality and birth, including the physical differences between males and females, sexual intercourse, and the birth of a baby. *(4–5)*

Before You Were Born *gives similar treatment to the development of a fetus, including its activities* in utero *and the process through which it gets food and oxygen from the mother.*

- Showers, Paul. **A Drop of Blood,** rev. ed. Illus. by Don Madden. Crowell (h) Harper (p) 1987. 32p col illus.

A simple introduction to blood, the role it plays in the body, how bleeding stops, and how the blood supply is replenished. *(5)*

The digestive and muscular systems are likewise treated in **What-**

Happens to a Hamburger *and* **You Can't Make a Move Without Your Muscles.**

- Showers, Paul. **Hear Your Heart.** Illus. by Joseph Low. Crowell (h) Harper (p) 1968. 35p col illus.

  The function of the human heart is explored with instructions for using a cardboard tube to listen to a heartbeat and for finding a pulse, and a discussion of how the heart rate varies due to age or activity. (5)

- Showers, Paul. **Look at Your Eyes.** Illus. by Paul Galdone. Crowell (h) Harper (p) 1962. unpaged col illus.

  As a small boy plays games looking in the car mirror, the functions of eyelids, lashes, pupils, and tears are demonstrated. (5)

  Follow Your Nose, How You Talk, *and* **How Many Teeth** *explore the sense of smell, speech, and teeth respectively.*

- Showers, Paul. **No Measles, No Mumps for Me.** Illus. by Harriet Barton. Crowell 1980. 33p col illus.

  A simple explanation is given of the bacteria and viruses that cause disease and how immunizations prepare the body to fight them. (5)

- Showers, Paul. **Sleep Is for Everyone.** Illus. by Wendy Watson. Crowell 1974. 33p col illus.

  Explains what happens when we sleep and why we need sleep. (5)

Transportation

- Barton, Bryon. **Airplanes.** Crowell 1986. unpaged col illus.

  A jet flies over a crop duster, a helicopter, and a seaplane, then lands and refuels before taking off again in this small book about flying.

  (0–5)

  Simple, brightly colored illustrations add to the appeal of this and the companion titles, **Trains, Trucks,** *and* **Boats.**

- Barton, Byron. **Airport.** Crowell (h) Harper (p) 1982. unpaged col illus.

  Minimal text and large colorful illustrations outline what happens from the arrival of a passenger at the airport until the departure of the plane.   *(2–5)*

- Crews, Donald. **Freight Train.** Greenwillow (h) Puffin (p) 1978. unpaged col illus.

  The various cars of a freight train are shown in different bright colors. The rhythmic text describes the journey. This has long-lasting appeal for train buffs.   *(1–5)*

- Crews, Donald. **Harbor.** Greenwillow 1982. unpaged col illus.

  Pictures of a busy blue harbor crowded with numerous colorful boats are accompanied by a minimal text; together they introduce different types of boats.   *(2–5)*

- Crews, Donald. **Truck.** Greenwillow (h) Puffin (p) 1978. unpaged col illus.

  A big, red truck travels out of the city, through a tunnel, over superhighways, and across a bridge to its final destination. Large illustrations in primary colors add to the appeal of this popular subject.
  (1–5)

  Gibbons, Gail. **Boat Book.** Holiday 1983. unpaged col illus.

  Boats serve a variety of purposes, from racing and other forms of recreation to performing hard work. Many types of boats and brief descriptions of their jobs are introduced in this book featuring accurate but uncluttered illustrations.
  (1–5)

- Gibbons, Gail. **Fill It Up! All About Service Stations.** Crowell (h) Harper (p) 1985. unpaged col illus.

  The reader is introduced to the many activities at a full-service gas station, including how a hydraulic lift works, how gasoline is pumped, and how a flat tire is fixed. A simple yet comprehensive and informative text is highlighted with bright illustrations.
  (3–5)

- Gibbons, Gail. **Trucks.** Crowell (h) Harper (p) 1981. unpaged col illus.

  Numerous brightly colored trucks are grouped by the type of work they do in this comprehensive book. Every truck is labeled, and detailed pictures show the work done by each one.
  (1–5)

- Maestro, Betsy. **Ferryboat.** Illus. by Giulio Maestro. Crowell 1986. unpaged col illus.

  A family's trip crossing a river on a ferryboat provides the focus for this picture book about an increasingly unusual form of transportation. Attractive watercolor illustrations show the river and ferryboat at different times of the day and in different seasons.
  (3–5)

- Provenson, Alice and Martin. **Glorious Flight: Across the Channel with Louis Bleriot.** Viking 1983. 39p col illus.

  In turn-of-the-century France, Louis Bleriot dreamed of building a flying machine. On his eleventh try, he succeeded in building one that flew across the English Channel. An understated text and impressionistic paintings present the glorious subject of flight and the many failures that often precede a successful invention. (5)

- Rockwell, Anne. **Cars.** Dutton (h&p) 1984. unpaged col illus.

  Race cars, vintage cars, and golf carts are among the types of cars included in this simple introduction to the automobile. Colorful, uncluttered illustrations show the different uses for cars and some of the many places they go. (1–5)

  Similar treatment is given to **Trucks, Big Wheels, Bikes, Boats,** *and* **Planes** *by the same author.*

- Rockwell, Anne. **Things That Go.** Dutton 1986. 24p col illus.

  A compendium of different vehicles and machines that move (including toys and sports equipment) grouped according to where they're used. Each item included is labeled and pictured with an animal character using it. (1–5)

Plants and Gardening

- Brown, Marc Tolon. **Your First Garden Book.** Little, Brown (h&p) 1981. 48p col illus.

  A lighthearted but accurate introduction to the pleasures and rewards of growing vegetables and flowers presents several gardening activities with a minimum of fuss. (2–5)

- Le Tord, Bijou. **Rabbit Seeds.** Macmillan/Four Winds 1984. unpaged b&w illus.

  Young children will meet with success if they follow the steps of this gardener rabbit: prepare the soil, plan, plant, weed, thin, and water. The appealing and helpful illustrations clearly show stages of plant growth and useful tools. (3–5)

- Miner, O. Irene Sevrey. **Plants We Know.** Childrens Press (h&p) 1981. 45p col photos.

  Plants are shown to be important for food as well as beauty. An easy text and color photographs introduce several common plants and the many benefits we derive from them, including food and aesthetic beauty. (5)

- Rush, Hanniford. **The Beginning Knowledge Book of Backyard Trees.** Illus. by Raul Mina Mora. Macmillan 1964. unpaged col illus.

  Eighteen commonly found trees are identified both in large pictures and in simple text. (4–5)

• Rylant, Cynthia. **This Year's Garden.** Illus. by Mary Szilagyi. Bradbury 1984. unpaged col illus.

The cycles of activity and waiting involved in the planning, planting, and harvesting of a year's garden are outlined in text and beautiful, richly colored illustrations. (3–5)

• Selsam, Millicent E. **More Potatoes.** Pictures by Ben Shecter. Harper 1972. 62p col illus.

In an easy-to-read format, this lively book traces the raising and marketing of potatoes. (4–5)

• Titherington, Jeanne. **Pumpkin Pumpkin.** Greenwillow 1986. 23p col illus.

Soft pencil drawings follow the planting of a pumpkin seed, its maturation, and the saving of its seeds to plant the following year. (2–5)

• Udry, Janice May. **A Tree Is Nice.** Illus. by Marc Simont. Harper (h&p) 1956. unpaged col and b&w illus.

Illustrations that sparkle with life and a simple, lyrical text celebrate the beauty, fun, and importance of trees. (2–5)

• Wexler, Jerome. **Flowers, Fruits, Seeds.** Prentice-Hall 1987. unpaged col photos.

Superb, well-labeled color photographs of various flowers, fruits, and seeds accompany an introduction to the characteristics and purposes of each featured item. (3–5)

A litter of wire-haired dachshunds is followed in a similar manner in **A Puppy Is Born.**

- Kuklin, Susan. **Taking My Cat to the Vet.** Bradbury 1988. unpaged col photos.

  A young boy accompanies his pet cat on a visit to the vet. The text, told from the child's point of view through his questions to the vet, describes the various procedures. Clear, relevant photographs complement the thorough text. (3–5)

  Similar treatment is given in **Taking My Dog to the Vet.** *Each includes a list of suggestions at the end for a successful visit to the vet.*

- Roy, Ron. **What Has Ten Legs and Eats Corn Flakes?** Illus. by Lynne Cherry. Clarion 1982. 48p b&w illus.

  Very young children have a hard time caring for traditional pets, but they can easily assume responsibility for the hermit crab, the American chameleon, and the gerbil, which need minimal and virtually identical attention. (3–5)

Pets

- Bare, Colleen Stanley. **Guinea Pigs Don't Read Books.** Dodd, Mead 1985. unpaged col photos.

  While they don't read books, guinea pigs are attractive little mammals, as the color photographs and brief text clearly show. (0–5)

- Brown, Ruth. **Our Cat Flossie.** Dutton 1986. unpaged col illus.

  Attractive color illustrations and a simple, understated text capture the true nature of cats by depicting Flossie, whose hobbies include bird watching and fishing but especially sleeping. (2–5)

- Brown, Ruth. **Our Puppy's Vacation.** Dutton 1987. unpaged col illus.

  Rich illustrations and simple text capture a young puppy's spunk and curiosity on vacation in the English countryside. (2–5)

- dePaola, Tomie. **The Kids' Cat Book.** Holiday (h&p) 1979. unpaged col illus.

  Patrick gets plenty of free advice about the many kinds of cats and a brief history of their relationship with humans, and learns how to care for a cat when he goes to Granny Twinkle for a free kitten. (4–5)

- Fischer-Nagel, Heiderose and Andreas. **A Kitten Is Born.** Putnam 1983. unpaged col photos.

  Follow the birth and development of three kittens through a flowing narrative and delightful color photographs. (3–5)

Backyard Animals

- Carle, Eric. **The Very Busy Spider.** Philomel 1985. unpaged col illus.

  Handsome and intriguing collage illustrations provide the background for the determination of a spider to finish her web despite the entreaties from the other farm animals for her to join them in their activities.

  (3–5)

  In **The Very Hungry Caterpillar** *a small caterpillar eats his way through several fruits and other foods until he is a huge caterpillar.*

- Dallinger, Jane. **Grasshoppers.** Photographs by Yuko Sato. Lerner 1981. 48p col photos.

  Grasshoppers can be both helpful and major pests, as this attractive photographic essay clearly documents. *(4–5)*

- Gans, Roma. **When Birds Change Their Feathers.** Illus. by Felicia Bond. Crowell 1980. 40p col illus.

  It's easy to collect feathers at the time birds molt, but why and how do they do it? Similarly, other animals lose their furs or skins or shells, and the simple text explains the process clearly. *(3–5)*

- Hawes, Judy. **My Daddy Longlegs.** Illus. by Walter Lorraine. Crowell 1972. unpaged col illus.

  The behavioral characteristics of this very popular insect are shown in attractive drawings and described in a simply written text. *(4–5)*

• Hurd, Edith Thacher. **Look for a Bird.** Pictures by Clement Hurd. Harper 1977. 30p col illus.

Become a bird watcher by looking out for these familiar backyard birds. The illustrations help show where to spot them, and the text provides some basic information about each of the thirteen species featured.

(2–5)

• Kaufmann, John. **Birds Are Flying.** Crowell 1979. 40p col illus.

Birds fly in different ways, as the easy-to-read text and drawings show. (2–5)

• McClung, Robert M. **Sphinx: The Story of a Caterpillar.** Illus. by Carol Lerner. Morrow 1981. unpaged b&w illus.

This narrative about the life cycle of a moth features superb pen drawings and an anthropomorphic text. (3–5)

• Myrick, Mildred. **Ants Are Fun.** Pictures by Arnold Lobel. Harper 1968. 63p col illus.

Trying to rebuild an ant nest gives three boys the chance to discover a variety of the behavioral and physiological traits of these busy insects.

(3–5)

• Reidel, Marlene. **From Egg to Butterfly.** Carolrhoda 1981. 24p col illus.

This small book explains the biological process of metamorphosis as applied to a butterfly in simple text and colorful illustrations. (3–5)

• Rossetti, Christina. **The Caterpillar.** Illus. by Debra Stine. Calico Books 1988. unpaged col illus.

A unique combination of verse and striking watercolor illustrations conveys considerable information about the life of a caterpillar in a board-book format. (1–3)

- Ryder, Joanne. **Fireflies.** Pictures by Don Bolognese. Harper 1977. 61p col illus.

  Dark summer evenings are regularly brightened by these small insects. The pleasant text supported by the attractive drawings traces their life cycle.   *(2–5)*

- Selsam, Millicent, and Joyce Hunt. **Keep Looking.** Illus. by Norman Chartier. Macmillan 1989. 32p col illus.

  A snow-covered house seems to be deserted, but careful observation reveals the signs of animal life all around it. The watercolor illustrations are lovely, and a brief index helps locate the animals again.   *(3–5)*

- Zeitlin, Patty, and Marcia Berman. **Spin, Spider, Spin.** Sung by Patty Zeitlin, Marcia Berman, and David Zeitlin; accompanied by David Zeitlin. B/B Records 1974. (Record/cassette). ⬤▣

  Learn to enjoy, rather than fear, common and harmless insects, arachnids, reptiles, and amphibians through these zestful songs. *(4–5)*

On the Farm

- Brandenberg, Franz. **Cock-a-Doodle-Doo.** Illus. by Aliki. Greenwillow 1986. unpaged col illus.

  A simple text and cheerful color illustrations show the animals and noises on a farm morning, including the farmer's "thank you" and the baby's "mmmmm." Prompts young children to join in. (1–3)

- Cole, Joanna. **Chick Hatches.** Photos by Jerome Wexler. Morrow 1977. 47p b&w photos.

  Look through an eggshell and watch a chick develop through superb photographs explained in a smooth text. (3–5)

- dePaola, Tomie. **"Charlie Needs a Cloak."** Prentice-Hall (h&p) 1974. unpaged col illus.

  The wool sheared, washed, carded, spun, woven, and dyed by Charlie the shepherd is made by him into a beautiful new cloak. (3–5)

- Freedman, Russell. **Farm Babies.** Holiday 1981. 38p b&w photos.

  Find out about typical farm animals through pleasant photographs and simple text. (3–5)

- Gibbons, Gail. **Farming.** Holiday 1988. unpaged col illus.

  The animals, equipment, and work done on the farm are shown through the seasons in labeled illustrations. (3–5)

- Gibbons, Gail. **The Milk Makers.** Macmillan (h&p) 1985. un-paged col illus.

  This simple book shows how milk gets from the cow on the farm to the carton on supermarket shelves. Bright diagrams help provide the information. *(4–5)*

- Ginsburg, Mirra. **Across the Stream.** Illus. by Nancy Tafuri. Greenwillow (h) Puffin (p) 1982. 23p col illus.

  Rhyming text tells how a duck and her ducklings save a hen and her chicks from a fox. The brightly colored large illustrations add to the fun. *(0–5)*

- Greely, Valerie. **Farm Animals.** Bedrick/Blackie 1985. unpaged col illus.

  Double-page realistic pictures show familiar farm animals. The sturdy board pages allow even the youngest to handle the book with ease.

  (1–3)

  Other titles in the series are **Zoo Animals, Pets,** *and* **Field Animals.**

- Hall, Donald. **Ox-Cart Man.** Illus. by Barbara Cooney. Viking (h) Puffin (p) 1979. unpaged col illus.

  A farmer in New England packs the cart with all the things his family has made throughout the year and takes them to market. The primi-tively styled pictures capture the flavor of the mid-1800s. *(4–5)*

  A read-along kit is available from Live Oak Media. ▪▪

- Hands, Hargrave. **Bunny Sees.** Grosset 1985. unpaged col illus.

  A board book that features double-page illustrations of a rabbit who sees a variety of other animals. The text is simple and repetitive, so young children can easily join in and name what the bunny sees. (1–3)

  The other titles in the series, **Little Lamb Sees, Duckling Sees, Puppy Sees,** *and* **Little Goat Sees,** *follow the same format.*

• Isenbart, Hans-Heinrich. **A Duckling Is Born.** Photos by Othmar Baumli. Putnam 1981. unpaged col photos.

Attractive color photographs follow a mallard family from courtship through the hatching of a nestful of baby ducklings. The text of the photographic essay is well written.   (4–5)

• Maris, Ron. **Is Anyone Home?** Greenwillow 1986. unpaged col illus.

A young child discovers who or what is behind various doors on Grandma and Grandpa's farm. Half pages allow the reader to open the doors and gates, and attractive watercolor illustrations with small details add to the game.   (1–3)

• Montgomery, Constance and Raymond. **Vermont Farm and the Sun.** Photos by Dennis Curran. Vermont Crossroads Press 1975. 32p b&w photos.

Clear, large, black-and-white photographs, many full page, combined with a simple text, portray farm life and an appreciation for the many forms of solar energy.   (2–5)

• Tafuri, Nancy. **Early Morning in the Barn.** Greenwillow (h) Puffin (p) 1983. unpaged col illus.

Early morning on the farm is hardly quiet, with the rooster crowing and the chicks, ducks, cows, and other animals adding their voices to his. The bright pictures contain some visual jokes that are fun to pick out.   (2–5)

• Tafuri, Nancy. **Have You Seen My Duckling?** Greenwillow (h) Puffin (p) 1984. unpaged col illus.

Count the ducklings, even the one that is hiding from mother duck.

(0–3)

In **Rabbit's Morning** *follow the young bunny as he hops around the meadow searching for food and meets other animals.*

• Wheeler, Cindy. **Rose.** Knopf 1985. unpaged col illus.

Told almost solely through its pictures, this is a hilarious tale of a pig who goes searching for a cooler spot and innocently causes bedlam.

(1–5)

Wild Animals

- Arnosky, Jim. **Watching Foxes.** Lothrop 1985. unpaged col illus.

  Color-pencil drawings show four fox cubs eagerly exploring their environment. The simple text and the drawings are based on first-hand observation. *(2–5)*

  Come Out, Muskrats *follows the animals as they swim, eat, and play in the pond each night.*

- Bonners, Susan. **Panda.** Delacorte 1978. unpaged col illus.

  Born in the mountains of south China, a young panda is followed from cubhood to motherhood. Lovely watercolor illustrations show her both in snow and living in the midst of bamboo groves. *(2–5)*

- Bonners, Susan. **Penguin Year.** Delacorte 1981. 44p col illus.

  The life cycle of the charming Adelie penguin is simply, informatively, and attractively presented. *(3–5)*

- Burton, Marilee Robin. **Tail Toes Eyes Ears Nose.** Harper 1989. unpaged col illus.

  The parts of an animal are shown on one page, followed on the next page by the whole animal. Then the tails from all the animals are shown together followed by all the different feet, the eyes, the ears, and the noses. The format provides a guessing game and is a source for comparing different animals. *(3–5)*

- Cooke, Ann. **Giraffes at Home.** Illus. by Robert Quackenbush. Crowell 1972. unpaged col illus.

  These favorite tall animals are seen in their native habitat, eating, raising their young, and protecting themselves and their young from predators. (3–5)

- Freedman, Russell. **Getting Born.** Holiday 1978. unpaged b&w photos.

  Whether they hatch out of eggs—frogs, turtles, chickens—or are born alive—dolphins, kittens, horses—the birth process is fascinating. (3–5)

- Goor, Ron and Nancy. **All Kinds of Feet.** Crowell 1984. 48p b&w photos.

  A bird has one type of foot, a monkey another, a horse another, and an elephant still another. By showing how the foot is related to function, the authors encourage observation. (5)

- Hirschi, Ron. **Who Lives in . . . the Forest.** Photos by Galen Burrell. Dodd, Mead 1987. unpaged col photos.

  Wander through the woods and meet some of the birds and other animals who live there through striking color photographs and a lyrical text. An afterword for parents tells where to look for the various animals featured. (3–5)

- Leen, Nina. **Rare and Unusual Animals.** Henry Holt 1981. 80p b&w photos.

  Striking closeup photographs present a number of less frequently seen animals. (3–5)

• McNulty, Faith. **Woodchuck.** Pictures by Joan Sandin. Harper 1974. 64p col illus.

A simply written text details the numerous events that comprise a female woodchuck's year, as she awakes from hibernation, finds a mate, and gives birth to four babies. (3–5)

• Selsam, Millicent E. **Hidden Animals.** Harper 1969. 63p b&w photos.

Animals use camouflage to hide from their predators, and the black-and-white photographs in this book challenge the reader to find the "hidden animals" as well. (3–5)

• Sheehan, Angela. **Beaver.** Illus. by Graham Allen. Warwick/ Watts 1979. unpaged col illus.

Building dams, gathering food, and raising kits are all part of the beaver's life and are described here in clear words and pictures. (5)

• Wildsmith, Brian. **Fishes.** Oxford (h&p) 1968. unpaged col illus.

Magnificent color illustrations of groups of different fishes (each described with an unusual collective noun—herd, flotilla, swarm) are presented in this lovely book. (1–5)

• Yoshida, Toshi. **Young Lions.** Philomel 1989. unpaged col illus.

Three lion cubs set off across the grassy African plain to hunt for food. The stunning color-pencil drawings dramatically capture the cubs' prey in flight. (2–5)

Dinosaurs

- Barton, Byron. **Dinosaurs, Dinosaurs.** Crowell 1989. unpaged col illus.

  Endpapers feature the nine different types of dinosaurs discussed in the very simple text. The illustrations are brightly colored and primitively styled. Use this as an introduction to the subject, then move on to more informative and detailed works. *(1–2)*

- Carrick, Carol. **Patrick's Dinosaurs.** Illus. by Donald Carrick. Clarion (h&p) 1983. unpaged col illus.

  Patrick's older brother describes dinosaurs so vividly that Patrick sees them everywhere. Though the story's format is fictional, the information is accurate, and the dramatic paintings help satisfy youngsters' enthusiasm for these prehistoric creatures. *(5)*

- Cohen, Daniel. **Dinosaurs.** Illus. by Jean Zallinger. Doubleday 1986. 41p col illus.

  This striking book contains a wealth of information accompanied by large, well-labeled illustrations of these perennially favorite creatures. Even two-year-olds can pronounce these monstrous names. *(4–5)*

- Gibbons, Gail. **Prehistoric Animals.** Holiday 1988. unpaged col illus.

  Through labeled pictures and a brief text, several prehistoric creatures are introduced. Some, which inhabited the earth after dinosaurs disappeared, are ancestors of today's animals. *(4–5)*

- Parish, Peggy. **Dinosaur Time.** Pictures by Arnold Lobel. Harper (h&p) 1974. 30p col illus.

  Although extinct, dinosaurs are popular with children. This simple text introduces eleven types and presents information about their size, food, and habits.   *(3–5)*

  A read-along kit is available from Random House. ▪▪

- Prelutsky, Jack. **Tyrannosaurus Was a Beast: Dinosaur Poems.** Illus. by Arnold Lobel. Greenwillow 1988. 32p col illus.

  Humor and information are brilliantly blended in fourteen poems about different dinosaurs.   *(3–5)*

- Selsam, Millicent E. **Sea Monsters of Long Ago.** Illus. by John Hamberger. Macmillan/Four Winds (h) Scholastic (p) 1978. 32p col illus.

  Reptile monsters lived in the sea when dinosaurs lived on earth. How and what scientists found out about them is described.   *(4–5)*

- Simon, Seymour. **The Smallest Dinosaurs.** Illus. by Anthony Rao. Crown 1982. 47p col illus.

  Possibly the forebears of today's birds, seven small dinosaurs are described in simple text and attractive drawings.   *(5)*

Earth and Outer Space

- Barton, Byron. **I Want to Be an Astronaut.** Crowell 1988. unpaged col illus.

  A young girl tells about her desire to be an astronaut aboard a space shuttle. Boldly colored illustrations defined with heavy black outlines complement the simple text. (3–5)

- Branley, Franklyn M. **Air Is All Around You**, rev. ed. Illus. by Holly Keller. Crowell (h) Harper (p) 1986. 32p col illus.

  While air can't be seen, its presence can be proven to young children with the simple experiments found in this good-looking slender book. (3–5)

  A read-along kit is available from Harper Audio. ▭

- Branley, Franklyn M. **Rain and Hail.** Illus. by Harriett Barton. Crowell 1983. 39p col illus.

  The cycle of water evaporating from the earth, forming clouds, and falling to earth again is given a lucid explanation, accompanied by colorful, fun illustrations. (3–5)

  Snow Is Falling, *illus. by Holly Keller, answers children's perpetual questions about snow.*

- Branley, Franklyn M. **The Sky Is Full of Stars.** Illus. by Felicia Bond. Crowell (h) Harper (p) 1981. 34p col illus.

  A new understanding of the night sky is provided by this book as it helps the reader to find and identify well-known constellations. Instructions are included for making pictures of the constellations using a flashlight and a coffee can. (3–5)

- Branley, Franklyn M. **Sunshine Makes the Seasons**, rev. ed. Illus. by Giulio Maestro. Crowell (h) Harper (p) 1985. 32p col illus.

  A clear, easily understood text answers children's questions about how the seasons change and why the length of the day changes through the year. An experiment with an orange, a stick, a pin, and a flashlight further demonstrates the reasons why the seasons change. (4–5)

  A read-along kit is available from Harper Audio. ▣

- Branley, Franklyn M. **What Makes Day and Night**, rev. ed. Illus. by Arthur Dorros. Crowell (h) Harper (p) 1986. 32p col illus.

  The earth's rotation causes day and night. An easy-to-do experiment featured in the book helps youngsters to understand this. (4–5)

- Branley, Franklyn M. **What the Moon is Like**, rev. ed. Illus. by True Kelley. Crowell (h) Harper (p) 1986. 32p col illus. and photos.

  Twelve astronauts have explored the moon. Readers of this book can find where the different expeditions landed, see the landscape of the moon, and gain basic information about its environment. (4–5)

  A read-along kit is available from Harper Audio. ▣

- dePaola, Tomie. **The Quicksand Book.** Holiday (h&p) 1977. 32p col illus.

  In his attempt to rescue Jungle Girl from quicksand, Jungle Boy finds himself mired in the stuff. The "recipe" for quicksand in the back of the book really works. (5)

- Engdahl, Sylvia Louise. **Our World Is Earth.** Illus. by Don Sibley. Atheneum 1979. unpaged col illus.

  Stunning full-page paintings provide the backdrop for this book's smooth narrative, which explains the life forms found on earth. (3–5)

• Gibbons, Gail. **Sun Up, Sun Down.** Harcourt 1983. unpaged col illus.

Bright pictures and simple narrative combine to show how the warmth of the sun and the light it gives contribute to life. (2–5)

• Lewellen, John Bryan. **Moon, Sun and Stars.** Childrens Press (h&p) 1981. 45p col photos.

Straightforward information about the force of gravity, the waxing and waning of the moon, and the planets are included in this small book. (4–5)

• Martin, Bill Jr., and John Archambault. **Listen to the Rain.** Illus. by James Endicott. Henry Holt 1988. unpaged col illus.

Highly stylized watercolor illustrations capture the essence of this paean to the sounds made by the stages of a rainstorm, from "the slow soft sprinkle" through "the hurly-burly topsy-turvy lashing gnashing teeth of rain." Wonderfully tactile language. (1–5)

• McNulty, Faith. **How to Dig a Hole to the Other Side of the World.** Illus. by Marc Simont. Harper 1979. 32p col illus.

The matter-of-fact tone of the narrative as the hypothetical young explorer is guided through the layers of the earth and told about the supplies that will be needed makes this informative book a delight. The illustrations help show just how hot the center of the earth really is. (4–5)

• Peters, Lisa Westberg. **The Sun, the Wind and the Rain.** Illus. by Ted Rand. Henry Holt 1988. unpaged col illus.

An understanding of the formation of a mountain is made accessible through parallel stories tracing the creation of two mountains: an earth-made one formed by shifting rock, wind, water, and time, and one made of sand by a girl on the beach. (4–5)

- Pollock, Penny. **Water Is Wet.** Photographs by Barbara Beirne. Putnam 1985. unpaged b&w photos.

  Water is wet and young children have a great deal of fun splashing and playing with it. (2–5)

- Simon, Seymour. **Earth: Our Planet in Space.** Macmillan/Four Winds 1984. unpaged b&w photos.

  Simple text, diagrams, and dramatic photographs show how earth's characteristics and position make it unique in the solar system. (5)

- Simon, Seymour. **Shadow Magic.** Illus. by Stella Ormai. Lothrop 1985. 48p col illus.

  Several activities involving shadow play (including sundials and shadow pictures) invite children to create and explore. (3–5)

- Tangborn, Wendell V. **Glaciers**, rev. ed. Illus. by Marc Simont. Crowell (h) Harper (p) 1988. 32p col illus.

  What are glaciers made of? Where are they found now? How do they move? How do they shape the earth? Simple narrative and attractive pictures answer these questions. (3–5)

- Ziner, Feenie, and Elizabeth Thompson. **Time.** Childrens Press (h&p) 1982. 45p col photos.

  A very basic introduction to telling time, introducing the many methods used for telling time through history as well as those currently used, including digital clocks. (4–5)

A Matter of Taste:
Developing Preferences

Adults need all their wits and energy to keep up with little children. As they start to gain possession of their world, little children display fertile imaginations, create their own adventures and mysteries, and look at the world from a very different and often hilarious perspective. Stories that fuel their creativity and reinforce their sense of the ridiculous are among their favorites.

Young children think it is funny to throw a toy out of a crib repeatedly. Adults don't find it amusing at all. So it is with the stories young children find funny. Their sense of humor borders the fine line between slapstick and corny. Try not to groan as you read the stories that send them into gales of giggles.

Mysteries and adventures for them are certainly mild when compared to adult books in the genre. It is sometimes hard for adults to realize that each day is greeted, rightfully, as an adventure by young children. A mystery is locating a misplaced toy or peering behind a tree. The tone of the books in these genres reflect this simplicity.

Sometimes young children have difficulty distinguishing between reality and fantasy. They think they can build a rocketship to outer space with the aid of a chair and a funnel. Many have imaginary friends. Watching them at play is a delight, because their creativity knows no boundaries.

Bear with the humor. Play along with the small mysteries and adventures. Encourage their ingenuity. Your day and the rest of their lives will be better for it.

Imagination

- Alexander, Martha. **Blackboard Bear.** Dial 1969. unpaged col illus.

  Told he's too small to play with the older boys, a young boy draws a big bear with a collar and leash on the blackboard. The bear comes down off the blackboard, and the boy takes him for a walk—but of course no one but the boy is allowed to play with the bear. (3–5)

- Asch, Frank. **Mooncake.** Prentice-Hall (h&p) 1983. unpaged col illus.

  Bear and his friend Little Bird are sure the moon is made of cake and long to taste it. The primitive strong-outlined, boldly colored illustrations add charm. (2–5)

- Bonsall, Crosby. **Tell Me Some More.** Pictures by Fritz Siebel. Harper 1961. 64p col illus.

  Tim discovers that books found in the public library can make all kinds of unlikely things happen. (3–5)

- Burningham, John. **Come Away from the Water, Shirley.** Crowell 1977. unpaged col illus.

  Shirley's parents tell her it's too cold for swimming at the beach. While they nonchalantly sit in beach chairs and tell her don't do this and don't do that, she goes out to sea, boards a pirate ship, and finds buried treasure. The juxtaposition of Shirley's parents calling to her on the left-hand page and her adventure, told entirely in pictures on the right-hand page, add the right touch of humor to this imaginative book. (2–5)

- Drescher, Henrik. **Simon's Book.** Lothrop (h) Scholastic (p) 1983. unpaged col illus.

  Stylized and angular illustrations accompany this story in which dreams and drawing come together in a book young Simon creates. Somewhat scary but nonetheless fun. (5)

- Hoban, Tana. **Look Again.** Macmillan 1971. unpaged b&w photos.

  Look at a bit of a photograph through a small frame. Can you tell what the object is? Though this book is entirely without words, it certainly sparks comments. (3–5)

  Take Another Look (Greenwillow) *provides nine more subjects to identify.*

- Holl, Adelaide. **Rain Puddle.** Illus. by Roger Duvoisin. Lothrop 1965. unpaged col illus.

  The reflective nature of a puddle sends animals, one by one, frantically seeking help for the animal each is positive is trapped. A variant on a popular theme. (2–5)

- Jensen, Virginia Allen. **Catching.** Philomel 1983. 23p col illus.

  Raised textual patterns are used to help tell the story of Little Rough, who changes his shape to fool his friends while they are playing tag. Designed originally for blind children, this is quite an unusual experience for sighted youngsters. (2–5)

- Johnson, Crockett. **Harold and the Purple Crayon.** Harper (h&p) 1955. unpaged col illus.

  A magical crayon transforms drawings to the real things a small boy needs for a moonlight walk. (2–5)

  The crayon comes through again when he decides to travel to the sky in

Harold's Trip to the Sky *and when he decides he needs an interesting picture in his room in* **A Picture for Harold's Room.**

- Jonas, Ann. **The Trek.** Greenwillow 1985. unpaged col illus.

  An ordinary walk to school becomes tense with adventure when a young girl becomes convinced that a chimney is a giraffe and that other wild animals are hiding along her way. The puzzle element in the double-page-spread watercolor paintings keeps youngsters and adults enthralled. (3–5)

- Kroll, Steven. **Tyrannosaurus Game.** Illus. by Tomie dePaola. Holiday (h&p) 1976. 39p col illus.

  Rainy days are bad enough, but rainy school days are even worse— until an old/new game transforms things. (5)

- Lionni, Leo. **Geraldine the Music Mouse.** Pantheon (h&p) 1979. unpaged col illus.

  Gnawing pieces off a large chunk of cheese to share with her friends, Geraldine creates a giant statue of a mouse playing the flute. The statue comes to life and plays beautiful music for Geraldine and her friends. (3–5)

- McClintock, Mike. **What Have I Got?** Pictures by Leonard Kessler. Harper 1961. 32p col illus.

  A young boy imagines the many things he could do with the everyday items in his pockets, including a ball, a piece of string, and a dish. (4–5)

- McPhail, David. **Bear's Toothache.** Little, Brown (h&p) 1972. 31p col illus.

  The howling of a bear suffering with a toothache awakens a small boy, who tries to help the bear pull the tooth. When the tooth does finally come out, the bear happily leaves the boy with a huge tooth to sleep with under his pillow. (5)

A read-along kit is available from Live Oak Media. ●●

- Murphy, Jill. **What Next, Baby Bear!** Dial (h&p) 1984. unpaged col and b&w illus.

It's bath time, but Baby Bear wants to go to the moon. He finds a box to use as a rocket and a colander as a helmet, packs food and his teddy bear, and flies up the chimney to the moon—returning in time for his bath. An imaginative story illustrated with full-page color illustrations and smaller black-and-white vignettes. (3–5)

- Scheer, Julian, and Marvin Bileck. **Rain Makes Applesauce.** Holiday 1964. unpaged col illus.

A series of silly statements illustrated with detailed double-page pictures to stretch the imagination. (3–5)

- Shub, Elizabeth. **Seeing Is Believing.** Illus. by Rachel Isadora. Greenwillow 1979. 63p illus.

Tom, a farm boy in County Cork, Ireland, longs to see the fairies and elves everyone talks about. He finally meets an elf and tries to get his gold, but the clever fellow outsmarts him. (4–5)

- Shulevitz, Uri. **One Monday Morning.** Aladdin (p) 1967. unpaged col illus.

On a dark, rainy morning in a New York tenement, a young boy daydreams of a king, a queen, a little prince, and their royal entourage dropping in to pay him a visit. (4–5)

- Van Allsburg, Chris. **Jumanji.** Houghton Mifflin 1981. unpaged b&w illus.

  Two children discover a board game called "Jumanji, A Jungle Adventure." One day when their parents are out, they decide to play it, with alarming and all-too-real results. Fantastic, vivid, black-and-white illustrations pull the viewer into the game, where fantasy and reality meet. (5)

- Yektai, Niki. **What's Missing?** Illus. by Susannah Ryan. Clarion 1987. unpaged col illus.

  Laughter may win out as youngsters try to figure out "what's missing," in this series of almost-normal pictures. (3- 5)

- Zelinsky, Paul O. **The Maid and the Mouse and the Odd-shaped House: A Story in Rhyme.** Dodd, Mead 1981. unpaged col illus.

  As a maid and her mouse make additions and changes to their odd-shaped house, they are unwittingly creating a huge cat from whom they must escape. (3–5)

Mystery and Adventure

- Ahlberg, Janet and Allan. **Funnybones.** Greenwillow 1981. unpaged col illus.

  Skeletons romp through a dark, dark town looking for someone to scare—and end up scaring each other just for fun. (2–5)

- Alexander, Sue. **World-Famous Muriel.** Illus. by Chris L. Demarest. Little, Brown (h) Dell (p) 1984. 48p col illus.

  Muriel is famous for tightrope walking and solving difficult mysteries. Lots of action and humor fill the comic-style illustrations and repetitive text. (3–5)

- Ardizzone, Edward. **Little Tim and the Brave Sea Captain.** Puffin (p) 1955. unpaged col illus.

  Discovered as a stowaway on board a steamer, Little Tim is forced to work. During a bad storm, the ship hits a rock and all escape except for Little Tim and the ship's captain. (5)

- Aylesworth, Jim. **Two Terrible Frights.** Illus. by Eileen Christelow. Atheneum 1987. unpaged col illus.

  Almost identical stories of a little girl and a little mouse are told on opposite pages as they each go to the kitchen for a bedtime snack and frighten one another. (3–5)

• Benchley, Nathaniel. **The Strange Disappearance of Arthur Cluck.** Illus. by Arnold Lobel. Harper (h&p) 1967. 64p col illus.

Mrs. Cluck's son Arthur is missing, and Ralph, the wise old barn owl, helps to solve the mystery of his disappearance. (3–5)

• Bunting, Eve. **Ghost's Hour, Spook's Hour.** Illus. by Donald Carrick. Clarion 1987. unpaged col illus.

Awakened by a noise in the middle of a night when the power has gone out, Jake and his dog Biff are frightened by the noises and images in the darkened house. Wonderful sound effects, spooky illustrations, and appropriate touches of humor frame this "scary" story that children request again and again. (3–5)

• Burningham, John. **Where's Julius?** Crown 1986. unpaged col illus.

As Julius journeys all over the world, his adoring parents always manage to bring his meals to him. Fascinating large color illustrations show Julius riding a camel up a pyramid, pouring water on a hippopotamus in Central Africa, throwing snowballs at Russian wolves, and watching a sunset from a mountaintop in Tibet. (3–5)

• Calhoun, Mary. **Cross-Country Cat.** Illus. by Erick Ingraham. Morrow (h) Mulberry (p) 1979. unpaged col illus.

Henry, a Siamese cat who can walk and dance on his hind legs, refuses to learn to ski until he is left behind at his family's ski lodge. There he not only learns how to ski but embarks on an adventure trying to find his way home. (4–5)

• Fox, Mem. **Hattie and the Fox.** Illus. by Patricia Mullins. Bradbury 1987. unpaged col illus.

Hattie the black hen sees a nose, two eyes, two legs, and a body in the bushes, but the other animals are unconcerned—until it turns out to be a fox. The cumulative story builds the suspense. Young children enjoy the animal chorus and the tissue-paper-collage illustrations. (1–4)

- Goodall, John S. **Jacko.** Harcourt (h&p) 1971. unpaged col illus.

  Jacko, an organ grinder's escaped monkey, goes to sea, where he encounters pirates and frees a caged parrot. The action-filled tale is told entirely through the richly colored pictures. (2–5)

- Hann, Jacquie. **Follow the Leader.** Crown 1982. unpaged col illus.

  A group of children follows a young girl into an old house, past a black cat and cobwebs, through a secret door, and into the attic, where there are bats and—ghosts! (3–5)

- Henkes, Kevin. **Sheila Rae, the Brave.** Greenwillow 1987. unpaged col illus.

  Constantly praising herself for her bravery, Sheila Rae is at a loss when she finds herself in totally foreign surroundings and must become dependent on her scaredy-cat sister Louise to get home. (3–5)

- Jonas, Ann. **Where Can It Be?** Greenwillow 1986. unpaged col illus.

  Readers open doors and pull back covers as a young girl looks all over the house for something. Then the doorbell rings and it's the girl's friend with—her blanket! Young children enjoy joining the seach by turning the pages and finally finding the beloved blanket. (1–3)

- Kellogg, Steven. **The Mystery of the Missing Red Mitten.** Dial (h&p) 1974. unpaged col illus.

  Annie and her dog, Oscar, attempt to solve the mystery of her missing red mitten. The mitten eventually turns up in a most unusual place. (2–5)

- Koide, Tan. **May We Sleep Here Tonight?** Illus. by Yasuko Koide. Atheneum/McElderry 1981. unpaged col illus.

  Lost in the fog in the woods, a series of small animals find shelter in a cabin and crawl into bed. Something huge and black comes in, and all are frightened until the benevolent identity of the stranger is revealed. Warm, gentle illustrations and a little suspense provide a slightly scary but reassuring story. (2–5)

- Lobel, Arnold. **Mouse Soup.** Harper (h&p) 1977. 63p col illus.

  Mouse convinces Weasel—who is about to cook him in a soup—that he needs some stories to make a really tasty mouse soup. Mouse tells several stories about bees, stones, crickets, and a thorn bush, and while Weasel goes in search of these ingredients for the soup, Mouse escapes. (4–5)

  As read-along is kit available from Harper Audio. ▪▪

- Marzollo, Jean and Claudio. **Jed's Junior Space Patrol.** Illus. by David S. Rose. Dial (h&p) 1982. 56p col illus.

  A simple, moderately suspenseful science-fiction story that includes a spaceship, space travel, robots, and animals called cogs that have the characteristics of both cats and dogs. (4–5)

- McCloskey, Robert. **Burt Dow, Deep-Water Man: A Tale of the Sea in the Classic Tradition.** Viking 1963. 61p col illus.

  An old fisherman catches a whale by the tale and uses a candy-striped Band-Aid to patch the hole in his boat in this tall tale illustrated with colorful, exuberant paintings. (2–5)

- Peet, Bill. **Cowardly Clyde.** Houghton Mifflin (h&p) 1979. 38p col illus.

  Cowardly Clyde is a large war-horse who only pretends to be brave. But when his master, Sir Galavant, is in trouble, Clyde overcomes his fear and ousts a monster that has been terrorizing the countryside. (4–5)

- Peet, Bill. **Jennifer and Josephine.** Houghton Mifflin 1967. 46p col illus.

When Jennifer, an old touring car, is bought from the junk yard by a "large, long-legged fellow with two suitcases and puffing a cigar," she and her cat friend Josephine take off on a reckless series of adventures.
(4–5)

- Rockwell, Anne and Harlow. **The Night We Slept Outside.** Macmillan 1983. 48p 2-color illus.

Two brothers sleep outside on their deck and try not to be frightened by a raccoon, a cat, a skunk, and an owl until a thunderstorm forces them inside.
(3–5)

- Steig, William. **Caleb & Kate.** Farrar (h&p) 1977. 32p col illus.

Walking out on his wife after a quarrel, Caleb falls asleep in the woods and is turned into a dog by a witch. He returns home to his wife, Kate, who doesn't recognize him but adopts the stray. His problem is finally resolved during an attempted robbery. A book that appeals on many different levels.
(3–5)

- Steig, William. **Roland the Minstrel Pig.** Harper 1968. 32p col illus.

Dreaming of fame and wealth, Roland decides to become a wandering minstrel. He meets up with a cunning fox, who plans to have him for dinner and convinces Roland that he will take him to sing for the king. After several unsuccessful attempts the fox is finally about to roast poor Roland when the king happens by and rescues him. Roland's voice and talent make him wealthy and famous in the king's court, while the fox ends up in jail with only bread, water, and sour grapes to eat. (4–5)

- Tafuri, Nancy. **The Ball Bounced.** Greenwillow 1989. unpaged col illus.

  A small boy drops a ball. This results in a flurry of activity as the ball bounces through the house and out the door. Bright, large illustrations capture the action and excitement. (1–2)

- Titherington, Jeanne. **Where Are You Going, Emma?** Greenwillow 1988. unpaged col illus.

  While on an apple-picking expedition with her grandfather, young Emma decides to climb the wall surrounding an orchard and has a mostly satisfying adventure. The soft colored-pencil drawings are wonderfully inviting. (3–5)

- Turkle, Brinton. **Do Not Open.** Dutton (h&p) 1981. unpaged col illus.

  Miss Moody and her cat, Captain Kidd, comb the beach for treasures after a violent storm and find a bottle marked "Do not open." Of course they open it and out pops a horrible monster. Miss Moody outwits the creature, and she and Captain Kidd return home. A satisfying story illustrated in rich, warm colors. (4–5)

- Zemach, Harve. **The Judge, an Untrue Tale.** With pictures by Margot Zemach. Farrar 1969. unpaged col illus.

  A judge sends five prisoners to jail for telling the untruth that "a horrible thing is coming this way, creeping closer day by day," but in the end he gets what he deserves for not believing them. Told in cumulative rhyme that has listeners joining in. (3–5)

Humor

- Allard, Harry. **I Will Not Go to Market Today.** Illus. by James Marshall. Dial (h&p) 1979. unpaged col illus.

  Fenimore B. Buttercrunch's trip to the market is delayed by a blizzard, a heat wave, dense fog, a hurricane, an earthquake, a flood, and finally a broken leg.   (3–5)

- Allen, Pamela. **Bertie and the Bear.** Coward McCann (h&p) 1984. unpaged col illus.

  Bertie is chased by a great big bear, who in turn is chased by the Queen, King, Admiral, Captain, General, Sergeant, and a small dog, each of whom makes a different noise. Hearing the commotion, the bear finally turns around, says, "Thank you," and leads them in a merry parade. Children enjoy the noise and the bright illustrations.
                                                                 (2–5)

- Aylesworth, Jim. **Hush Up!** Illus. by Glen Rounds. Henry Holt 1980. unpaged col illus.

  The cacaphony of the cat, hound, pig, rooster, billy goat, and mule awaken Jasper Walker from a serene nap.   (2–5)

- Bonners, Susan. **Just in Passing.** Lothrop 1989. unpaged col illus.

  Yawns are contagious, as this wordless story humorously illustrates.
                                                                 (2–5)

- Brown, Marc Tolon, and Laurene Krasny Brown. **Bionic Bunny Show.** Little, Brown (h&p) 1984. 31p col illus.

  Colorful, cartoonlike illustrations and deadpan text provide an informative and funny look behind the scenes of a television show starring a superhero. A glossary of television terms is included. (4–5)

- Burningham, John. **Mr. Gumpy's Outing.** Henry Holt (h) Puffin (p) 1970. unpaged col illus.

  Mr. Gumpy decides to go for a boat ride. One by one, several children and animals ask to join him, promising they'll behave. But eventually things get out of hand, and they all get wet. (2–5)

  In the sequel, **Mr. Gumpy's Motor Car**—*Crowell (h), Puffin (p)—Mr. Gumpy and his human and animal friends go for a ride in his touring car.*

- Duke, Kate. **Bedtime.** Dutton 1986. unpaged col illus.

  A young guinea pig unrolls the toilet paper, watches bubbles from the bathtub, squeezes out the toothpaste, pulls all the books off the shelves, and finally settles down for bed. Typical toddler activity is depicted in these humorous board books featuring guinea pigs. (1–2)

  Other titles are **The Playground, Clean-Up Day,** *and* **What Bounces?**

- Geringer, Laura. **A Three Hat Day.** Illus. by Arnold Lobel. Harper (h&p) 1985. 30p col illus.

  R. R. Pottle the Third collects hats. When he's happy, he wears one hat. When he's unhappy, he wears two hats. One day, when he's very unhappy, he wears three. To cheer himself up, he goes into a hat store and there meets Isabel, who's wearing a most wonderful hat. They marry. When R. R. Pottle the Fourth is born, she doesn't care for hats. But she loves shoes. (4–5)

- Gretz, Susanna. **Hide-and-Seek.** Macmillan/Four Winds 1986. unpaged col illus.

  At bedtime Louise tries out several hiding places before she finds one that's not only comfortable but is the last place anyone would look—in her bed. Humorous bright-colored illustrations highlight the brief story in this board book. (1–3)

- Kellogg, Steven. **Pinkerton, Behave.** Dial (h&p) 1979. unpaged col illus.

  Pinkerton, the Great Dane puppy, is sent to obedience school but won't learn the commands; in fact he is a bad influence on the other members of the class. However, even though he's been sent home in disgrace, he does manage to successfully rout a burglar. (3–5)

  In **A Rose for Pinkerton** *his owners get him a kitten for companionship, which causes chaos at the International Pet Show. In* **Tallyho Pinkerton!** *a little girl's homework assignment takes her and Pinkerton out into the woods, where Pinkerton disrupts a fox-hunting class.* **Prehistoric Pinkerton** *finds the teething pup at the natural-history museum, where the dinosaur skeleton proves to be totally irresistible.*

- Leaf, Munro. **Wee Gillis.** Illus. by Robert Lawson. Viking 1938. unpaged b&w illus.

  Wee Gillis is caught in the middle of the rivalry between his father's Highlander family and his mother's Lowlander family. To his and their astonishment he succeeds in besting both when he is the only one able to blow the enormous bagpipes. (3–5)

- Lobel, Arnold. **The Rose in My Garden.** Illus. by Anita Lobel. Greenwillow (h) Scholastic (p) 1984. unpaged col illus.

  The types of flowers blooming in a garden are described one by one in cumulative verse with lush illustrations. The visual interaction of a bee, a field mouse, and a cat, not mentioned in the text, add humor. (2–5)

- Mahy, Margaret. **Jam, a True Story.** Illus. by Helen Craig. Joy Street/Little, Brown 1985. unpaged col illus.

  Mr. and Mrs. Castle have three children. She works as an atomic scientist while he stays home and takes care of the children and the housework. One day the fruit on the plum tree ripens, and Mr. Castle makes jam until he has filled every container in the house with the stuff. All year long they eat jam, dream about jam, and, when the roof leaks, even use jam to patch it. A sweetly humorous story. (3–5)

- Mayer, Mercer. **A Boy, a Dog and a Frog.** Dial (h&p) 1967. unpaged brown-and-white illus.

  A boy and his dog attempt to trap a frog, who has ideas of his own in this hilarious wordless book. (3–5)

  Further humorous and wordless adventures occur in **Frog on His Own, Frog Goes to Dinner,** *and* **Frog Where Are You?**

- Mosel, Arlene. **Tikki Tikki Tembo.** Illus. by Blair Lent. Henry Holt (h&p) 1967. 40p col illus.

  Tikki tikki tembo-no sa rembo-chari bari ruchi-pip peri pembo is the name of a small Chinese boy. When he falls into a well, his younger brother is hampered in trying to get help because it takes so long to recite his brother's name. Children love the humor and enjoy chanting the long name. (3–5)

- Noble, Trinka Hakes. **The Day Jimmy's Boa Ate the Wash.** Illus. by Steven Kellogg. Dial (h&p) 1980. unpaged col illus.

  The class trip to the farm was boring except for the cow crying, the haystack falling over, the pigs on the school bus, and the egg fight—all because Jimmy brought his pet snake along. (4–5)

  In **Jimmy's Boa Bounces Back,** *the snake disrupts a garden club meeting.*

- Palmer, Helen. **A Fish Out of Water.** Illus. by P. D. Eastman. Random House 1961. 64p col illus.

  A young boy ignores the shopkeeper's warning about feeding and gives his new fish the entire box of food. Problems soon follow when the fish grows too big for any container the boy has. This is a humorous and easy-to-read story. (4–5)

- Raskin, Ellen. **Ghost in a Four-Room Apartment.** Atheneum (p) 1969. unpaged col illus.

  The poltergeist who visits Horace Homecoming causes chaos as bells ring, blocks fly, furniture sails, and cupboards seem to explode while ever-increasing numbers of Horace's family watch. (4–5)

- Rayner, Mary. **Mr. and Mrs. Pig's Evening Out.** Atheneum (h&p) 1976. 32p col illus.

  The agency sitter's plans to turn Garth Pig into a snack is foiled by the cleverness of the other nine piglets, who save their brother and throw disguised Mrs. Wolf into the river. (4–5)

  In **Garth Pig and the Ice Cream Lady** *she's foiled again by the piglets on their bicycle built for ten. In* **Mrs. Pig's Bulk Buy** *the piglets' mother gives them their favorite ketchup for breakfast, lunch, snacks, and dinner.*

- Seligson, Susan, and Howie Schneider. **Amos: The Story of an Old Dog and His Couch.** Joy Street/Little, Brown 1987. unpaged col illus.

  Amos is an old dog who spends most of his time on a couch. Then he discovers that he can drive the old couch as if it were a car. The wry illustrations and farfetched story are a delight for adults and children to share. (3–5)

- Small, David. **Imogene's Antlers.** Crown (h&p) 1985. 32p col illus.

  Imogene wakes up one morning with antlers. Her mother faints and her brother makes wisecracks, but she finds that the unusual headgear often comes in handy. (4–5)

- Spier, Peter. **Bored—Nothing to Do.** Doubleday (h&p) 1978. unpaged col illus.

  Bored, two brothers build an airplane from things around the house— and it flies! Their parents are perplexed when nothing around the house works and numerous things are missing until they discover their sons' invention. Imaginatively and humorously depicted almost entirely in pictures. (4–5)

- Steig, William. **Doctor De Soto.** Farrar (h) Scholastic (p) 1982. unpaged col illus.

  Doctor De Soto, a dentist, and his wife are mice, so they have a policy of staying away from the mouths of dangerous animals. But they make an almost fatal exception for a fox in excruciating pain. (3–5)

  A read-along kit is available from Scholastic. ▪▪

- Stevenson, James. **What's Under My Bed?** Greenwillow (h) Penguin (p) 1983. unpaged col illus.

  Mary Ann and Louie run downstairs to Grandpa because they are afraid of the terrible things that lurk under their beds. Grandpa tells them about the monsters, skeletons, and goblins that lived under his bed when he was a boy. A humorous tall tale told in comic-book style. (3–5)

  Similar humor occurs in **We Can't Sleep** *and* **Could Be Worse.**

- Suteyev, Vladimir. **The Chick and the Duckling.** Translated from the Russian by Mirra Ginsburg. Illus. by Jose Aruego and Adriane Dewey. Macmillan (h&p) 1972. unpaged col illus.

  Hatched at the same time, a duckling and a chick become constant companions until the chick's attempt to follow the duckling into the water almost ends in disaster. When the duckling decides to go for another swim, the chick's "Me too" changes to "Not me." Bright, humorous illustrations pair with simple text. (2–5)

- Waber, Bernard. **The House on East 88th Street.** Houghton Mifflin (h&p) 1962. 48p col illus.

When the Primm family moves into a new apartment, they hear strange noises coming from the bathroom. They discover Lyle the crocodile, who with his wonderful antics soon becomes a beloved member of the household. (3–5)

There is a series of books about the Primms and Lyle, and a lilting recording available on cassette and record, **Lyle Crocodile and Other Adventures of Lyle,** *read by Gwen Verdon (Harper Audio).* ⊙ ▢▢

- Westcott, Nadine Bernard. **Giant Vegetable Garden.** Atlantic/ Little, Brown (h&p) 1981. 31p col illus.

Believing that big is better, the mayor and townspeople of Peapack work hard to grow the biggest vegetables for the county fair. They do win the prize for the "Best Vegetable," but their huge vegetables have overrun the small town. (3–5)

- Wood, Audrey. **King Bidgood's in the Bathtub.** Illus. by Don Wood. Harcourt 1985. unpaged col illus.

King Bidgood won't get out of the bathtub. All who try to convince him to get out end up in the tub with him (completely dressed in their royal best)—until a young page literally pulls the plug. (3–5)

A cassette recording (one side read-along, the other cast into a delightful operetta) is available from Random House/Miller Brody. ▢▢

- Wood, Audrey. **The Napping House.** Illus. by Don Wood. Harcourt 1984. unpaged col illus.

On a rainy day the sleeping inhabitants of a napping house pile on top of each other one by one. Then a wide-awake flea bites a sleeping mouse and begins a chain of events that awakens everyone to bright sunshine and a rainbow. Humorous illustrations accompany the cumulative story. (2–5)

- Zion, Gene. **Harry the Dirty Dog.** Pictures by Margaret Bloy Graham. Harper (h&p) 1956. unpaged col illus.

  Harry is a white dog with black spots who runs away because he hates baths. He has a great time getting into all kinds of messes, but returns home so dirty that his family doesn't know him until he convinces them to give him a bath. (2–5)

  Harry's adventures continue in **No Roses for Harry, Harry and the Lady Next Door,** *and* **Harry By the Sea,** *available in hardcover and paperback.*

  All except **No Roses For Harry** *are available as read-along kits from Random House.* ▪▪

Special Times

Young children are always doing. It seems hard to believe that they could ever run out of things to do. Yet sometimes their activity needs direction or a change of pace. Holidays and the changing seasons provide the occasion for enjoying numerous activities together: reading special stories and poems; learning seasonal music and creating appropriate handicrafts and recipes.

At other times simple science experiments, games, or musical recreations provide needed breaks in the routine, for you as well as them. At all times music and singing are welcomed and enjoyed by youngsters. The great thing about singing with young children is that you don't have to worry about singing on key. They love it no matter how tone deaf you think you are.

Holidays and Seasons

- **American Christmas.** National Geographic 1977. (Record/cassette) ● ▥

  This recording features popular Christmas songs, including "Hark, the Herald Angels Sing," "The Twelve Days of Christmas," "We Wish You a Merry Christmas," and "Deck the Halls." (2–5)

- Brand, Oscar, and Friends. **Your Birthday Party.** Harper Audio 1986. (Record/cassette) ● ▥

  Celebrate birthdays in fourteen languages. Each song is introduced with comments by Oscar Brand on the different birthday traditions. (3–5)

- Briggs, Raymond. **The Snowman.** Random House (h&p) 1978. unpaged col illus.

  A young boy's snowman comes to life. The boy brings the snowman inside and introduces him to the many modern conveniences, including running water, television, electricity, and dentures. Glowing illustrations tell the wordless story. (2–5)

- Bunting, Eve. **St. Patrick's Day in the Morning.** Illus. by Jan Brett. Clarion (h&p) 1980. unpaged col illus.

  Jamie gets up early on St. Patrick's Day, dresses in holiday regalia, and marches to the ceremonial stage, where he places the Irish flag. (4–5)

- Bunting, Eve. **Scary, Scary Halloween.** Illus. by Jan Brett. Clarion (h&p) 1987. unpaged col illus.

  A spooky poem is accompanied by vivid illustrations of jack-o'-lanterns, ghosts, and other seasonal creatures. The suspense builds until the end, when the surprising narrators are revealed. Just right for the season.

(3–5)

- Carlson, Natalie Savage. **Spooky and the Ghost Cat.** Illus. by Andrew Glass. Lothrop 1985. unpaged col illus.

Spooky, a black cat, breaks a witch's spell and changes a white ghost cat into a family pet. Eerie illustrations add to the holiday appeal.

(3–5)

- Caudill, Rebecca. **A Certain Small Shepherd.** Illus. by William Pène du Bois. Henry Holt (h&p) 1965. 48p col illus.

Jamie, who has never spoken a word, is disappointed when a snowstorm cancels the Christmas Nativity play in which he was to portray a shepherd. When a young couple seeks shelter from the storm on Christmas Eve, Jamie has an opportunity to be a part of a different Christmas miracle. *(4–5)*

- Clifton, Lucille. **The Boy Who Didn't Believe in Spring.** Illus. by Brinton Turkle. Dutton (h&p) 1973. unpaged col illus.

King Shabazz—who wears an Afro and shades—doesn't believe spring is just around the corner. He and his friend Tony Polito set out to find spring and finally find signs of the season in a trash-strewn vacant lot.

(5)

- Cole, Brock. **The Winter Wren.** Farrar (h&p) 1984. unpaged col illus.

Simon and his sister are looking for Spring but find chilly Old Man Winter, who turns Meg into a bird. Simon must release Spring to free his sister from Winter's spell. Beautiful watercolor illustrations capture the mood of the story. *(5)*

- Crews, Donald. **Parade.** Greenwillow (h) Mulberry (p) 1983. unpaged col illus.

  Full-color, cheerful pictures capture the excitement and fun of a parade. (2–5)

- Dabcovich, Lydia. **Sleepy Bear.** Dutton (h&p) 1982. 32p col illus.

  Large illustrations show the seasons changing as bear grows sleepy in autumn, sleeps through winter, and awakens to birds, bees, and bugs in spring. (1–5)

- Florian, Douglas. **A Year in the Country.** Greenwillow 1989. unpaged col illus.

  Double-page-spread illustrations show how life in the country changes month by month. (2–5)

- Friedrich, Priscilla and Otto. **The Easter Bunny that Overslept.** Illus. by Adrienne Adams. Lothrop (h) Mulberry (p) 1983. unpaged col illus.

  One year the Easter Bunny sleeps past Easter and tries to deliver his eggs on the Fourth of July and Halloween. Finally he meets Santa Claus, who gives him an alarm clock so he won't oversleep again.

  (2–5)

- Gibbons, Gail. **Christmas Time.** Holiday (h&p) 1982. unpaged col illus.

  Decorations, gift giving, the Biblical Christmas story, and Santa Claus are some of the aspects of this holiday explained in a simple text with colorful illustrations. (3–5)

  Other titles by the same author give similar treatment to the back-

grounds and customs for the holidays **Halloween, Thanksgiving Day,** *and* **Valentine's Day.**

Read-along kits are available for each of the titles from Live Oak Media. **◖◗**

- Hayes, Sarah. **Happy Christmas, Gemma.** Illus. by Jan Ormerod. Lothrop 1986. unpaged col illus.

  Gemma's older brother describes his family's preparation and celebration of Christmas. This includes "help" from Gemma, who takes the decorations off the tree, puts her bowl on her head, and eats the icing off Grandma's cake. Colorful illustrations picture the warmth and joy of one black family's Christmas. (2–5)

- Heyward, DuBose. **The Country Bunny and the Little Gold Shoes.** Pictures by Marjorie Flack. Houghton Mifflin (h&p) 1939. unpaged col illus.

  Cottontail persuades Grandfather Bunny that her skills as the mother of 21 children qualify her to be one of his five specially chosen Easter Bunnies. (4–5)

- Hirsh, Marilyn. **I Love Hanukkah.** Holiday (h&p) 1984. unpaged col illus.

  A small boy tells about celebrating Hanukkah with his family—learning about the history of the holiday, lighting the menorah, eating potato pancakes, and playing with a dreidel. (3–5)

  I Love Passover (1985) *gives similar treatment to this Jewish holiday.*

- Joosse, Barbara. **Fourth of July.** Illus. by Emily Arnold McCully. Knopf 1985. unpaged col illus.

  "Wait until you are six" is the refrain five-year-old Ross hears constantly. As he carries the banner in the Fourth of July parade, he is

determined to behave like a six-year-old would and earn some of the privileges of the age group. (5)

- Keats, Ezra Jack. **The Snowy Day.** Viking (h) Puffin (p) 1963. 32p col illus.

  The excitement and joy a small boy experiences in a snowfall are expressed in simple words and striking collage illustrations. (1–5)

- Kessel, Joyce K. **Halloween.** Illus. by Nancy L. Carlson. Carolrhoda 1980. 48p 2-color illus.

  The Celtic, Irish, and Roman origins of Halloween customs—such as trick-or-treating, jack-o-lanterns, and bobbing for apples—provide the historical basis for our current celebration of the holiday. (3–5)

- Kessel, Joyce K. **Squanto and the First Thanksgiving.** Illus. by Lisa Donze. Carolrhoda 1983. 47p b&w illus.

  This easily read book describes the events leading up to the first Thanksgiving by focusing on the life of the Indian Squanto and his relationship to the European settlers. (4–5)

- Livingston, Myra Cohn. **Thanksgiving Poems.** Illus. by Stephen Gammell. Holiday 1985. 32p col illus.

  Moving poems about the history and religious aspects of the holiday, and humorous, joyous poems about the feasting and celebration, comprise this balanced collection. (4–5)

- Marshall, Edward. **Space Case.** Illus. by James Marshall. Dial (h&p) 1980. unpaged col illus.

  A thing from Outer Space lands on earth on Halloween, and the children who are trick-or-treating think he's a kid with a great costume. (2–5)

In **Merry Christmas, Space Case** *by James Marshall, Buddie wonders if the outer space visitor will be able to find him at his grandmother's house.*

- McNaughton, Colin. **Autumn.** Dial 1984. unpaged col illus.

  Familiar fall activities are depicted with few words and charming, bright illustrations in this board book. (0–3)

  The other seasons are introduced in a similar manner in **Spring, Summer,** *and* **Winter.**

- Modell, Frank. **One Zillion Valentines.** Greenwillow (h) Mulberry (p) 1981. unpaged col illus.

  Marvin and Melvin never get any valentines because they never send any, so they decide to make a zillion. After giving one to everyone they know, they still have a zillion so they sell them and buy each other a big valentine. The humor is enhanced with comical illustrations. (3–5)

- Raffi. **Raffi's Christmas Album.** With Ken Whiteley. Kimbo 1983. (Record/cassette) ❶ 🄲🄾

  Raffi exuberantly performs many of the classic children's favorites for the holiday, including "Jingle Bells," "Frosty the Snowman," and "Rudolph, the Red-nosed Reindeer." (2–5)

- Robbins, Ken. **Beach Days.** Viking 1987. unpaged col photos.

  Hand-tinted photographs of Windsurfers, sand castles, children eating and playing, and the seemingly endless sand and sea capture the mood of the beach in summer. (2–5)

- Rockwell, Anne. **First Comes Spring.** Crowell 1985. unpaged col illus.

  Bear child demonstrates the appropriate clothing for a particular season.

His appearance is followed by a double-page panorama of the towns-people involved in seasonal activities, and the question, "What are they doing?" Turn the page, and detailed captioned pictures identify the activities. (2–5)

• Rockwell, Anne and Harlow. **The First Snowfall.** Macmillan 1987. unpaged col illus.

After snow falls one night, a young girl goes out to shovel snow, build a snowman, and ride a sled. Simple text and illustrations highlight the events on a snowy day. (1–3)

In **My Spring Robin** *(by Anne Rockwell; illus. by Harlow Rockwell and Lizzy Rockwell) a small girl finds many signs of spring as she searches for a returning robin.*

• Shachtman, Tom. **Parade!** Photos by Chuck Saaf. Macmillan 1985. 61p col photos.

Large color photos and informative text provide a behind-the-scenes look at a popular Thanksgiving tradition, the Macy's Thanksgiving Day parade. (4–5)

• Spier, Peter. **Christmas.** Doubleday (h&p) 1983. unpaged col illus.

Detailed color pictures capture the busy preparations, the celebrations on Christmas day, and the clean-up after the holiday. Children will pore over the detailed pictures in this wordless book. (2–5)

• Stevenson, James. **That Terrible Halloween Night.** Greenwillow 1980. unpaged col illus.

Grandpa tells Mary Ann and Louie about a Halloween night when he was a boy. He went into an old house that was so scary, he came out looking like an old man. A tall tale with just the right blend of humor and scariness. (3–5)

In **The Great Big Especially Beautiful Easter Egg** *Grandpa tells another tall tale about his long trip to the Frammistan Mountains to get an Easter egg for Charlotte, his heartthrob.*

- Van Allsburg, Chris. **The Polar Express.** Houghton Mifflin 1985. unpaged col illus.

  A young child boards a train to the North Pole, where he is chosen to receive the first gift of Christmas. He asks for a bell from Santa's reindeer. Deep-colored pastel drawings capture the mystery and excitement of Christmas and the emotions of childhood. **(4–5)**

- Vincent, Gabrielle. **Merry Christmas, Ernest and Celestine.** Greenwillow 1984. unpaged col illus.

  Ernest and Celestine throw a wonderful Christmas party for their friends. Affectionately told with soft-colored illustrations. **(4–5)**

- Wells, Rosemary. **Max's Christmas.** Dial 1986. unpaged col illus.

  A delightful pair, Max and his big sister, Ruby (from the board books), are featured in this picture book in which Max sneaks down to wait for Santa and meets a long-eared version of this character. **(2–5)**

  In **Max's Chocolate Chicken** *the irrepressible young rabbit puts acorns, a spoon, and ants in his basket rather than Easter eggs. Still, he's determined to get the chocolate chicken prize anyway.*

- Wells, Rosemary. **Morris's Disappearing Bag.** Dial (h&p) 1975. unpaged col illus.

  Morris is told he's too young to play with his brother's and sister's Christmas presents, until they discover he has a magical disappearing bag that everyone wants to take turns playing with. A delightful holiday fantasy in which the youngest sibling has something the older ones want enough that they'll share their own presents. **(4–5)**

- Zolotow, Charlotte. **Over and Over.** Illus. by Garth Williams. Harper 1957. unpaged col illus.

A little girl has a difficult time remembering the days of the week and the months. After each holiday she asks her mother what's next, and her mother tells her Christmas, Valentine's Day, Easter, summer vacation, Halloween, Thanksgiving, and finally her birthday. Simply describes the holidays and the order in which they come with attractive color illustrations. (3–5)

Activities

- Ahlberg, Janet and Allan. **Each Peach Pear Plum: An "I Spy" Story.** Viking (h) Scholastic (p) 1978. unpaged col illus.

  Familiar characters from nursery rhymes and stories are hidden within detailed watercolor illustrations, creating an "I Spy" game. (3–5)

- Allen, Pamela. **Mr. Archimedes' Bath.** Lothrop 1980. unpaged col illus.

  Mr. Archimedes learns about volume and the displacement of water as he and his friends get in and out of the bath. (5)

- Anno, Mitsumasa. **Anno's Faces.** Philomel 1989. unpaged col illus.

  Ordinary fruits and vegetables are transformed with smiles and frowns, found on two clear plastic strips that can be placed over the page. An accurate introduction to fruits and vegetables extended into hours of fun with the faces. (2–5)

- Aruego, Jose, and Ariane Dewey. **We Hide, You Seek.** Greenwillow 1979. unpaged col illus.

  Find rhino and his African animal friends as they play hide and seek in this introduction to animal camouflage. (3–5)

- Branley, Franklyn M. **High Sounds, Low Sounds.** Illus. by Paul Galdone. Crowell 1967. unpaged col illus.

  How are different sounds created? and How do we hear sounds? are among the questions answered in this lucid and attractive introduction to the world of sound. Simple experiments involving common, everyday objects allow for firsthand exploration. (4–5)

- Brown, Laurene Krasny, and Marc Tolon Brown. **Dinosaurs Travel.** Joy Street/Little Brown 1988. 32p col illus.

  From getting ready for a trip through different ways to travel, this cheerful guide focuses on the adventure and fun of a journey. (3–5)

- Brown, Marc Tolan. **Hand Rhymes.** Dutton 1985. unpaged col illus.

  Fourteen action-filled rhymes are delightfully illustrated in full color. Each rhyme is also accompanied by small, boxed illustrations demonstrating hand motions for each line of the rhyme. (5)

  One of a series including **Play Rhymes, Party Rhymes,** *and* **Finger Rhymes.**

- Brown, Marcia. **Touch Will Tell.** Watts 1979. unpaged col photos.

  A "hands-on" introduction to learning about the world around us is provided through the sense of touch introduced in this book. Illustrated with striking color photographs (2–5)

- Chernoff, Goldie Taub. **Easy Costumes You Don't Have to Sew.** Costumes designed and illus. by Margaret A. Hartelius. Macmillan/Four Winds 1975. 41p col illus.

  Diagrams and simple instructions are provided for constructing several easy costumes using five basic techniques that require no sewing. The needed materials are likely to be found in the home. (3–5)

• Cobb, Vicki. **Lots of Rot.** Illus. by Brian Schatell. Lippincott (h) Harper (p) 1981. 35p col illus.

Mold, mildew, and bacteria are the types of rot introduced in this book. Includes several hands-on experiments involving decaying fruit, moldy bread, and dirty socks. (5)

• Crews, Donald. **Carousel.** Greenwillow 1982. unpaged col illus.

Using a special photographic technique with color paintings, the artist creates the illusion of sound and motion as a carousel begins, goes faster and faster, then slows down again. (2–5)

• Gibbons, Gail. **Playgrounds.** Holiday 1985. unpaged col illus.

The sliding board, swings, seesaw, and other familiar pieces of playground equipment are all pictured with children playing on them in bold-colored illustrations with a simple text. (2–5)

• Gibbons, Gail. **The Pottery Place.** Harcourt 1987. unpaged col illus.

The author's stylized pictures and simple text describe the work of a potter: mixing the clay, working the potter's wheel, firing the pottery, and glazing it. Clay is a favorite medium of children, and the last page gives instructions for making a pinch pot, coil pot, and slab pot. (3–5)

• Gregson, Bob. **The Incredible Indoor Games Book: 160 Group Projects, Games, and Activities.** Pitman Learning (p) 1982. 187p b&w illus.

A compendium of games to play inside, ranging from simple ones requiring little or no equipment to more complex ones involving preparation and materials. (5)

• Hill, Eric. **Where's Spot?** Putnam 1980. unpaged col illus.

A very simple lift-the-flap book invites children to search for Spot the dog behind various doors and other openings and chime in with the repetitive text. Reinforce the flaps with tape to extend the life of this book. *(0–2)*

- Hoguet, Susan Ramsey. **I Unpacked My Grandmother's Trunk: A Picturebook Game.** Dutton 1983. 58p col illus.

  Colorful, imaginative illustrations depict this traditional alphabet memory game. Includes directions for playing the game without the book. *(3–5)*

- Kelley, True. **Look, Baby! Listen, Baby! Do, Baby!** Dutton 1987. unpaged col illus.

  Small, active illustrations depict a variety of babies involved in numerous babyhood activities. Babies will enjoy sharing the activities with an adult, and the heavy pages will hold up to repeated browsings by older youngsters. *(0–3)*

- Kunhardt, Dorothy. **Pat the Bunny.** Golden/Western. unpaged col illus.

  Patting the fuzzy bunny and lifting a flap of fabric to play peek-a-boo are among the many activities children are invited to share with Paul and Judy. Sturdy cardboard pages and spiral binding make this an easy book for youngsters to flip through. Be prepared to purchase second or third copies of this beloved book, because it will get heavy use. *(0–2)*

- Maris, Ron. **Are You There, Bear?** Greenwillow (h) Puffin (p) 1985. 32p col illus.

  One by one the unseen narrator illuminates many familiar toys with a flashlight while searching for Bear in a dark room. Children enjoy joining the search in the camouflaged pictures. *(2–5)*

- Rockwell, Anne. **Games (and How to Play Them).** Crowell 1973. 43p col illus.

  Full-color, playful illustrations accompany directions for 43 common group games in an accessible picture-book format. (3–5)

- Russo, Marisabina. **The Line-Up Book.** Greenwillow 1986. un-paged col illus.

  Lining up his blocks, books, bath toys, boots, cars, and trucks, and finally stretching out on the floor himself, Sam manages to span the distance from his room to the kitchen while his mother calls him for lunch. Simple yet eye-catching illustrations accompany this story about putting items in a line and problem solving. (2–5)

- Simon, Seymour. **Soap Bubble Magic.** Illus. by Stella Ormai. Lothrop 1985. 48p col illus.

  Blowing soap bubbles is a favorite activity of children. Numerous simple activities are suggested in this book to explore the many characteristics of soap bubbles while having fun creating them. (3–5)

- Webb, Angela. **Talkabout Reflections.** Photos by Chris Fair-clough. Watts 1988. unpaged col photos.

  The curious child will enjoy this introduction to reflections, to what sorts of objects make reflections, and to how the shape of the reflecting surface changes the reflected image. Includes activities involving mirrors to explore some of the properties of reflections. (3–5)

- White, Laurence B. **Science Toys and Tricks.** Illus. by Marc Tolon Brown. Lippincott (h) Harper (p) 1980. unpaged col illus.

  The curiosity and playfulness of young children is encouraged through several simple scientific activities. Large illustrations and easy-to-follow directions using basic household objects make this a very inviting book. (4–5)

  The companion volume, **Science Games and Puzzles,** *follows the same format.*

- Williams, Vera B. **Three Days on a River in a Red Canoe.** Greenwillow (h&p) 1981. unpaged col illus.

  A young girl tells about the camping and canoe trip she, her mother, her cousin, and her aunt took. Detailed, crayoned, childlike illustrations accompany her descriptions of the preparation and packing, and the adventure-filled trip. Recipes and directions for tying a half-hitch knot and setting up a tent are included. (3–5)

- Ziefert, Harriet. **Sarah's Questions.** Illus. by Susan Bonners. Lothrop 1986. unpaged col illus.

  Sarah and her mother take a walk and play "I Spy" along the way. Sarah asks a lot of questions—such as why squirrels have bushy tails and why birds sing—and receives straightforward and factual answers from her mother. Lush illustrations encourage observation as Sarah's mother fosters Sarah's curiosity about the world around her. (4–5)

Music and Songs

- **The Baby Record.** Featuring Bob McGrath and Katherine Smithrim. Kids' Records 1983. (Record).⦿

  Bouncing rhymes, finger plays, and lullabies make up this collection of activity songs. Clear instructions for each activity are included on the recording. *(0–2)*

- Bley, Edgar S. **The Best Singing Games for Children of All Ages.** Drawings by Patt Willen. Piano arrangements by Margaret Chase. Sterling (p) 1957. 96p b&w illus music.

  The author has collected musical scores and directions for games to play along with more than fifty folk and nursery songs. *(3–5)*

- Chapin, Tom. **Family Tree.** A&M Records 1988. (Record/cassette) ⦿ ▣

  Some silly songs, some serious songs, and some truly beautiful songs—on subjects that range from the environment to bedtime—address many of the concerns of children and their families. Judy Collins adds sparkle to three of the songs with her crystal-clear voice, and children's voices are also included in many of the selections. *(3–5)*

- Conover, Chris. **Six Little Ducks.** Crowell 1976. 32p col illus.

  In this picture book, detailed illustrations humorously expand the song about the one little duck with the feather in his back and his merry followers. *(1–5)*

- Dukas, Paul. **The Sorcerer's Apprentice.** Conducted by Leonard Bernstein; performed by the New York Philharmonic. Columbia. (Record). **O**

This collection of popular program music includes, in addition to the title piece, Mussorgsky's A Night on Bald Mountain, *Saint-Saens's* Danse Macabre, *and* Till Eulenspiegels Lustige Streiche *by Richard Strauss.*   (3–5)

- Fink, Cathy. **Grandma Slid Down the Mountain.** Rounder 1984. (Record/cassette). **O ▥**

A spirited collection of traditional song is combined with an activity book that includes lyrics and suggestions for accompanying activities involving sound effects, yodeling, clapping, and dancing.

(2–5)

- Fox, Dan, editor and arranger. **Go In and Out the Window.** Commentary by Claude Marks. Metropolitan Museum of Art/ Henry Holt 1987. 144p col illus.

This collection of familiar childhood songs is lavishly illustrated throughout with paintings, sculpture, and other objets d'art from the Metropolitan Museum of Art. A wonderful pairing of art with music and an ideal choice for sharing with all ages.   (0–5)

- Glazer, Tom. **Eye Winker, Chin Chopper: Fifty Musical Finger-plays.** Illus. by Ron Himler. Doubleday (h&p) 1973. 91p b&w illus.

Children love to join in songs, not only with their voices, but also by making motions with their fingers, hands, and arms. The words, music, and instructions for accompanying fingerplays for several familiar and some original songs are featured in this anthology.   (1–5)

Fourteen of the songs from **Eye Winker, Chin Chopper** *are performed by Tom Glazer, with instructions for the fingerplays on the recording* **Let's Sing Fingerplays** *(CMS).*

• Glazer, Tom. **Music for Ones and Twos.** CMS 1972. (Record/
cassette) ● ▣

Original songs and variations of familiar songs especially suited for
young children are introduced and sung by the inimitable Tom Glazer
on this recording and its sequel, **More Music for Ones and Twos.**

(1–3)

• Glazer, Tom. **Activity and Game Songs: vol. 1–3.** CMS 1973.
(Record/cassette) ● ▣

Young children form the audience for these lively recorded concerts.
Each song is given an introduction, and often children participate. The
enthusiasm of the young audience is contagious, and the listener can't
resist joining in with the fun. Volumes one and two contain many
perennial favorites, such as "Jennie Jenkins," "Put your Finger in the
Air," and "Rocky Candy Mountain." Volume three contains less
familiar folksongs, including several from other cultures.　　*(1–5)*

• Hurd, Thacher. **Mama Don't Allow.** Harper (h&p) 1984. unpaged col illus.

Miles and his Swamp Band are invited to play for the alligators' ball.
Only quick thinking and soft music keep them off the dinner menu.
Loud, colorful illustrations create the mood.　　*(2–5)*

• **If You're Happy and You Know It Sing Along with Bob:**
Preschool's Greatest Hits with Bob McGrath, Vols. 1 & 2. Kids'
Records 1984. (Record/cassette) ● ▣

A comprehensive selection of the most popular children's songs, both
contemporary and traditional, is sung in a clear voice by Sesame
Street's Bob McGrath.　　*(1–5)*

- Jenkins, Ella. **You'll Sing a Song and I'll Sing a Song.** Smithsonian Folkways dist. by Rounder (Record/cassette) ⦿⬚

Ella Jenkins is joined by children's voices in fifteen songs, including the title song, "Miss Mary Mack Mack," and "The Maori Indian Battle Chant," that encourage rhythm.

Other records by this popular artist and composer, who was a pioneer in music for children, include **Rhythms of Childhood** *and* **Little Johnny Brown.** (3–5)

- Kovalski, Maryann. **The Wheels on the Bus.** Joy Street/Little Brown 1987. unpaged col illus.

Grandma takes Jenny and Joanna shopping, and while waiting for the bus they sing the well-known title song. They get so involved in singing that they miss the bus. This rollicking rendition of the popular song is amusingly illustrated with a double-decker London bus. (1–5)

- Kuskin, Karla. **The Philharmonic Gets Dressed.** Illus. by Marc Simont. Harper (h&p) 1982. unpaged col illus.

This funny picture book shows how the 105 musicians of the Philharmonic prepare for a concert. Children love the detailed pictures of the musicians showering, shaving, dressing, and traveling to the concert hall. A humorous and informative behind the scenes look at the members of an orchestra. (4–5)

- Langstaff, John. **Frog Went A-Courtin'.** Pictures by Feodor Rojankovsky. Harcourt (p) 1955. unpaged col illus music.

The familiar ballad about the courtship and wedding of Frog and Miss Mousie is colorfully illustrated with fantastic pictures of the many insect and animal guests who are elaborately dressed for the occasion. (5)

Two other folk songs retold by the same author are **Oh, A-Hunting We Will Go,** *illus. by Nancy Winslow Parker (Atheneum) and* **Over in the Meadow,** *illus. by Feodor Rojankovsky (Harcourt).*

- Langstaff, John. **Let's Make Music.** Revels 1986. (Record/cassette) ⦿ ▣

The first side of this recording features four story-songs, including "Frog Went A-Courtin'" and "Over in the Meadow." Side Two invites children to participate by singing, playing a musical instrument, or inventing new verses to several folk songs. (3–5)

The recording **Songs for Singing Children** *is a collection of nursery rhymes, folk songs, and singing games.*

- Mack, Stanley. **10 Bears in My Bed: A Goodnight Countdown.** Pantheon 1974. 28p col illus.

A small boy finds ten bears in his bed and one by one tells them to "Roll over!" They empty his room of toy horses, trains, skates, and other toys as they gallop, chug, and skate out. (5)

Other presentations of this old counting song include **Roll Over!** *by Mordicai Gerstein (Crown) and* **Roll Over: A Counting Song** *by Merle Peek (Clarion).*

- Marxer, Marcy. **Jump Children.** Rounder Records 1986. (Record/cassette) ⦿ ▣

This lively, upbeat production features reggae or jazz beats on several songs. The reggae "Hush Little Baby" is a mesmerizing variation on this standard children's song. Many of the songs, including the title "Jump Children," invite children to get up and move around. Anyone listening to this recording will have a difficult time sitting still. (2–5)

- McCutcheon, John. **Mail Myself to You.** Rounder Records 1988. (Record/cassette) ⦿ ▣

Children's voices, hammer dulcimer, and ham bone are among the many wonderful sounds featured on this delightful album. The selection of songs includes the traditional "Over in the Meadow," two songs written by students in a special-education class, one song written with the performer's son on a car trip, the title song by Woody Guthrie, and "Turn Around," a beautiful song about the passing of childhood by Malvina Reynolds. Lyrics are included in a coloring book. (2–5)

- Parkinson, Kathy. **The Farmer in the Dell.** Whitman 1988. unpaged col illus.

The familiar song is illustrated with the story of a farmer who has a wife who has a child who has a nurse, and so on. The attractive format and clean design make singing along enjoyable. (1–4)

- Palmer, Hap. **Pretend.** Educational Activities 1975. (Record/ cassette) ●■■

Twelve short songs on the first side of this recording suggest numerous activities to act out: being a rag doll, playing a guitar, rushing, flying a kite, or jumping like a frog. The second side is instrumental, so children can imagine for themselves what the music suggests. Hap Palmer has been popular with teachers for several years, and many of his albums are most appropriate for classroom use. Among those suitable for using at home are two albums, **Baby Songs** *and* **Tickly Toddle,** *that feature songs on subjects of interest to very young children.* (2–5)

- Penner, Fred. **A House for Me.** A&M Records 1985. (Record/ cassette) ●■■

Seventeen songs, many traditional and familiar, are sung in a pleasant voice accompanied by a wide variety of instruments. Ken Whiteley, who also performs with Raffi, played a major role in the production of this recording, which is comparable in quality to Raffi's work. (2–5)

- Peter, Paul and Mary. **Peter, Paul and Mommy.** Warner Brothers. (Record/cassette) ●■■

The familiar folksinging group Peter, Paul and Mary harmonize on several songs for children, including "Day Is Done," "I Have a Song to Sing, O!" and the beloved "Puff the Magic Dragon." This older selection is still available and is timeless in its ability to weave a story in song or create a mood in music. (2–5)

• Prokofiev, Sergei. **Peter and the Wolf.** Performed by Carol Channing and the Cincinnati Pops Orchestra. Harper Audio. (Record/cassette) ◐▣

*The program-music favorite of Peter and his animal friends, the bird and the cat who succeed in trapping the fierce wolf, is engagingly narrated. The reverse side, **Tubby the Tuba,** is a delightful introduction to the sounds and sections of the orchestra through the tale of a tuba who longs to have a melody to play.* (3–5)

• Prokofiev, Sergei. **Peter and the Wolf.** New York Philharmonic; Leonard Bernstein conducting and narrating. Columbia. (Record/cassette) ◐▣

Sprightly program music retells the Russian folktale of the boy who, with the help of animal friends, captures a fierce wolf. (2–5)

*The story line has been placed in book form in two particularly notable interpretations: **Peter and the Wolf,** translated by Maria Carlson; illus. by Charles Mikolaycak—Viking (h) Puffin (p) 1982—has vigorous, detailed, and richly colored illustrations, and is excellent when read against the background of the music.*

***Peter and the Wolf,** illus. by Erna Voight (Godine 1980) provides a visual association between character and instrument at the beginning of the story. Relevant musical phrases are interspersed throughout the work along with stylish full-page illustrations.*

• Raffi. **The Corner Grocery Store and Other Singable Songs.** Sung by Raffi with Ken Whiteley. Kimbo 1979. (Record/cassette). ● ▣
Raffi's infectious style and clear voice encourage children to sing along with traditional and original songs. (0–5)

Other popular Raffi recordings are **Baby Beluga; Rise and Shine; Singable Songs for the Very Young; More Singable Songs; One Light, One Sun;** *and* **Everything Grows.** *Each contains a mix of traditional and newer songs and includes lyric sheets to facilitate singing along.*

• Raffi. **Down by the Bay.** Illus. by Nadine Bernard Westcott. Crown (h&p) 1987. unpaged col illus.

Raffi's songs are plenty of fun by themselves but the illustrations in this and **Shake My Sillies Out,** *illustrated by David Allender add even more hilarity. The music is included on the last page.* (2–5)

• Reynolds, Malvina. **Marcia Berman Sings Malvina Reynolds' Rabbits Dance and Other Songs for Children.** B/B Records 1985. (Record/cassette) ● ▣

A collection of affirmative and upbeat songs for children, on topics ranging from rabbits to Hanukkah to dancing, glowingly sung by Marcia Berman. (2–5)

• Rosenshontz. **It's the Truth.** RS Records 1984. (Record/cassette) ● ▣
Peppy, humorous songs about telling the truth, friendship, and the need for love and affection are featured in this collection. (3–5)

Other noteworthy albums by this duo: **Share It!** *and* **Tickles You!**

• Rosenthal, Phil. **Turkey in the Straw: Bluegrass Songs for Children.** American Melody Records 1985. (Record) **O**

The distinctive sound of this form of folk music is introduced through the original song "Listen to the Bluegrass," which highlights the various instruments. Several other more familiar and traditional songs are included on the album.   *(1–5)*

• Scruggs, Joe. **Traffic Jams.** Educational Graphics 1985. (Record/ cassette) **O DO**

Recordings are a hit with children on car trips. This upbeat collection includes several songs specifically about traveling in a car. It also features songs with activities to do in a car seat.   *(1–5)*

Other funny, toe-tapping albums by this artist include **Deep in the Jungle, Abracadabra,** *and* **Late Last Night.**

• Seeger, Pete. **American Folk Songs for Children.** Smithsonian Folkways dist. by Rounder 1954. (Record/cassette) **O DO**

Much of America's heritage of folk music is preserved on recordings for children by Pete Seeger. His old-timey voice and banjo picking add an authentic sound to this recording and three others: **Folk Songs for Young People; Birds, Beasts, Bugs and Little Fishes,** *and* **Birds, Beasts, Bugs and Bigger Fishes.**   *(1–5)*

• Seeger, Ruth Crawford. **American Folk Songs for Children in Home, School and Nursery School: A Book for Children, Parents and Teachers.** Illus. by Barbara Cooney. Doubleday (p) 1948. 190p b&w illus music.

The rich heritage of American folk music is found in this extensive collection. Numerous suggestions for improvisations, fingerplays, and other ways to use the songs are included. Musical notation is included. Peggy and Mike Seeger, two of Ruth Seeger's grown children, perform songs from this classic book on the recording **American Folk Songs for Children** *(Rounder Records).***O**   *(1–5)*

- Sharon, Lois and Bram. **One Elephant, Deux Elephants.** Elephant Records 1978. (Record/cassette)) ⭘ 𝄇

  Hand clapping, thigh slapping, whistling, and the voices of children are featured on this eclectic collection of 32 American and Canadian songs and playground chants. (3–5)

  There are numerous other recordings by this popular Canadian trio.

- **Songs & Games for Toddlers.** Featuring Bob McGrath and Katharine Smithrim. Kids' Records 1985. (Record/cassette) ⭘ 𝄇

  This is an inviting collection of activity songs and rhymes. Instructions for the activities are incorporated into the recording, and songs are often repeated to encourage the listener to sing and play along. (1–3)

- Spier, Peter. **The Fox Went Out on a Chilly Night: An Old Song.** Doubleday/Zephyr (p) unpaged col and b&w illus.

  Delightfully detailed and active illustrations of the Connecticut River Valley are the background for the lyrics of the long-popular folksong. The musical notation for piano and guitar and a recapitulation of the lyrics are at the end. (0–5)

- Tickle Tune Typhoon. **Circle Around.** Tickle Tune Typhoon 1983. (Record/cassette) ⭘ 𝄇

  Appealing subjects such as vegetables and dinosaurs are featured in these primarily original songs set to contemporary, upbeat music. This and the recordings **Hug the Earth** *and* **All of Us Will Shine** *contain songs with peppy lyrics and music that address the concerns of children with directness and humor.* (2–5)

- Van Manen, Dave and Helene. **Barley Bread and Reindeer Milk.** The Van Manens 1987. (Cassette) 𝄇

  This unique recording features many songs with the theme of world peace and fosters preschoolers' growing awareness of a larger world with many different kinds of people. Other songs deal with subjects closer to home, such as bedtime and "warm fuzzies," or comfort objects. All of the songs are enjoyable to listen to and fun to sing along with. *(4–5)*

- Weiss, Nicki. **If You're Happy and You Know It: Eighteen Songs Set to Pictures.** Greenwillow 1987. 40p col illus.

  Familiar songs like "Do Your Ears Hang Low?" "Pop Goes the Weasel," and "Hush Little Baby" are amusingly and thoroughly illustrated in this bright picture book. Musical notation for the songs is also included. *(1–5)*

- Westcott, Nadine Bernard. **I Know an Old Lady Who Swallowed a Fly.** Little, Brown (h&p) 1980. unpaged col illus.

  Read aloud or sing out loud this uproarious interpretation of the familiar nonsense song. The music for the song is included. *(2–5)*

Author, Illustrator, Performer Index

Title Index